Southwark

revisited

The Obelisk

Southwark

revisited

John D. Beasley

TEMPUS

Frontispiece: *A clock tower dominated St George's Circus, c. 1910.*

First published 2004

Tempus Publishing Limited
The Mill, Brimscombe Port,
Stroud, Gloucestershire, GL5 2QG
www.tempus-publishing.com

British Library Cataloguing in Publication Data.
A catalogue record for this book is available from the British Library.

ISBN 0 7524 3375 X

Typesetting and origination by Tempus Publishing Limited.
Printed in Great Britain.

Contents

Acknowledgements

Tribute must be paid to countless people, some known, but mostly unknown, who took pictures and recorded information. Without them this book could not have been compiled. In particular, thanks go to the following for pictures: South East Co-op Archive (p. 19), Salvation Army (p. 41), Charterhouse-in-Southwark (p. 46), Peckham Settlement (p. 53), Sons of Temperance Friendly Society (p. 55), Dr Alan Turberfield (p. 68), Friends of Nunhead Cemetery (p. 70), Independent Press Ltd (p. 71), pictorialpress.com (pp. 75 and 99), F.A. Albin & Sons (p. 76), W.A. Hammond (p. 83), Marjorie Foote (p. 87), Frank Staples (p. 119), Gary Cummins (p. 120) and Roy Brooke (p. 125).

Special thanks go to the excellent Southwark Local Studies Library and its talented staff – Ruth Jenkins, Stephen Humphrey, Steve Potter and Bob Askew. In particular much gratitude goes to the archivist and author Stephen Humphrey who read all the articles and made helpful suggestions prior to publication. Without the library, which is an invaluable resource, this book could not have been produced. Most of the pictures in *Southwark Revisited* were loaned by the library.

Sincere thanks also go to the *South London Press* for asking me in 1997 to write a weekly historical article on the London Borough of Southwark. In particular I am very grateful to a former editor, Rob Bowden, who originally commissioned me to write the articles but I also greatly appreciate the present editor, Hannah Walker, wanting me to continue writing articles for the South London Memories page in the Friday edition.

Introduction

It is rare to find a Roman inscription on an archaeological site but one unearthed in Southwark in 2002 was among the most important ever found in London. It was discovered buried in a pit on a development site between Long Lane and Tabard Street.

This fragmentary piece might have come from a temple or public building nearby. It is often difficult to interpret Roman stone inscriptions accurately due to damage and to the sculptor's use of abbreviated or imprecisely known Latin words.

The stone is particularly significant as it bears a very rare reference by name to Roman London. Its discovery in Southwark suggested that the Roman bridgehead settlement on the south bank of the Thames ranked as part of the City.

Since Roman times there have been amazing changes on the land south of the River Thames that from 1965 has been the London Borough of Southwark. Former old parishes and delightful Surrey villages are now included in London's most historic borough.

In 1865, one hundred years before the London Borough of Southwark was established, the *South London Press* was founded and since then has been writing stories about this area. As its editors have recognised Southwark's historical importance, the newspaper has published many articles on Southwark's intriguing and interesting history since 1997. My previous book *Southwark Remembered* and this book *Southwark Revisited* contain most of the 300 articles I have written for them in the last seven years.

Just as Romans came to the area, so Southwark is home to people who originated in many countries around the globe. As residents and visitors learn more about this fascinating London borough, the more interesting they will find their surroundings; knowledge of local history brings dull streets to life.

It is an absorbing experience to travel around Southwark knowing its exciting history. As a Yorkshireman brought up in Lincolnshire, who has lived in the borough for more than half my life, I find it enriching to have so many opportunities to learn about its past especially as history was a subject I hated (and came bottom of the class in!) when I was at school in Grimsby.

John D. Beasley
September 2004

The River Thames was frozen on 11 February 1895.

Dog Kennel Hill has a place in transport history. Tram tracks were laid in 1906 and the number of tracks was later increased to four for safety reasons so no trams could follow each other on the same line. Although other instances of four-lane tracks occur in the British Isles, Dog Kennel Hill was the only permanent arrangement.

one

Commerce

The former Leather Market is now used by other businesses.

The Leather Market was opened in Bermondsey in 1833. The building can be seen in Weston Street; it is now used by other businesses. In *The Buildings of England – London 2: South* Bridget Cherry and Nikolaus Pevsner describe it as 'a dignified building of stock brick with giant pilasters in the centre, and arched doorways at the ends (one surviving) for the vans to drive in'. Next door stands the grandiose London Leather, Hide & Wool Exchange, built forty-five years later. The origins of Bermondsey's leather trade date back to the fifteenth century. Tanning needs large amounts of running water so this work could be done because several tidal streams crossed the marshes and fields of Bermondsey. Tannin came from the bark of oak trees. The Thames-side wharves and the City's merchants and markets just across the river helped the leather trade to become established in Bermondsey. The Statute of Leather, which was passed in the early seventeenth century, broke the City's centuries-old monopoly on dealing in leather. It also authorised Southwark Fair as a place for the sale of leather. This was held in Borough High Street every September. Queen Anne granted the leather industry a charter in 1703. The Leather Market, erected by the Leather Warehouse Co. 130 years later, became the centre of the trade. Bermondsey's leather trade began to decline in the late nineteenth century but the last tannery did not close until well after the Second World War. The Market and Exchange were saved from destruction in 1993 when they were bought by the Workspace Group. Sympathetic conversion ensured that many of the original features have been preserved. Most of the 600 people who work at The Leather Market are engaged in design and consultancy.

A part from early examples of vinegar produced as a by-product of brewhouses, the first vinegar yard in Britain is said to have been in operation in Castle Street, Southwark, in 1641. In the years that followed, a number of fairly large companies grew up around the vinegar brewing industry. Sarson's, which had a factory in Tower Bridge Road, Bermondsey, traced its history back to 1794. Its name is the only one to have survived from the early days of the British vinegar industry; others disappeared as a result of mergers and acquisitions. British Vinegars Ltd, which was by far the largest vinegar brewer in the country, was formed in 1932 after several companies, including Sarson's, pooled their resources. 'Don't say Vinegar, say Sarson's' is a well-known slogan promoted by the firm. The traditional way to make vinegar was to stand tubs of ale or wine in the open air, allowing it to actify naturally. Louis Pasteur, best known as the father of pasteurisation, helped move production methods forward when he and some colleagues discovered the part bacteria played in the souring of wine. Sarson's was sited close to various breweries. There was a vinegar yard on the site of Sarson's from 1814. British Vinegars Ltd was acquired by the Swiss Nestlé group in 1979 and continued to manufacture a range of malt, distilled and speciality vinegars under the Sarson's trade name until 1992 when the site closed. The premises has since been converted into apartments. A watercolour drawing of Sarson's Vinegar Factory features in *Bermondsey and Rotherhithe Perceived* by Peter Marcan. A Buildings Recording (Industrial Processes and Photographic) Survey of the factory site can be seen at Southwark Local Studies Library, as can Steven Harris' *Old Surviving Firms of South London*, which includes Sarson's.

The rear of Sarson's vinegar factory was photographed here in 1988.

The Co-op store in Bermondsey sold a wide range of goods in 1959.

The Co-op store in Southwark Park Road, Bermondsey, opened on 9 September 1955. It belonged to the Royal Arsenal Co-operative Society but is now part of the Co-operative Group. The *South London Press* carried a large advertisement on the day the store opened. In design, layout and range of departments it was the first store of its kind in the district. It started off in a big way with hundreds of bargains and competitions with attractive prizes. The site was originally planned to house twelve separate shops. The RACS acquired the lot and decided to dispense with the dividing walls. The result was a spacious store with drapery, men's wear, footwear, furnishing, hardware, radio and electrical, and economy departments all on the ground floor. Flats occupied the first floor with the exception of a portion that was used as an extension to the furniture showrooms. For months RACS buyers hounded manufacturers and wholesalers, searching for bargains to be offered to customers at the new store. Before the store opened, a RACS photographer roamed the streets of Bermondsey snapping groups of people. The photographs were displayed in the store and vouchers worth £1, to be spent in any department, were waiting for fifty of the people in the pictures. Special opening bargains included: curtain nets at 2s a yard; blouses for 10s; children's blazers for 10s instead of 25s; men's Derby boots 37s 6d; 2ft 6in divans, complete with headboard and spring interior mattress, £11 19s 6d (normally £15 19s 6d); enamelled fry pans 2s 11d.

Old pictures of Co-op stores in Southwark Park Road are included in *The Co-operative Way* by Ron Roffey.

The year after this photograph was taken in 1966, Edgington's old premises were closed.

John Edgington & Co. Ltd was founded in 1805 and specialised in tent, rope and sail making. The company made the 'flags' of the rigging for Nelson's flagship. The explorers David Livingstone and Captain Robert Scott both bought their tents from the firm. Their premises were in the Old Kent Road. A plaque on the shop front recorded: 'Hereabouts in 1552 was erected a tent of cloth of gold for King Henry VIII and Charles V, the Holy Roman Emperor, before their entry into the City of London'. A picture above the doorway depicted the scene. The *Gentleman's Magazine* in 1838 recorded: 'Feb. 9. Messrs. Edgington's tarpauling and sail manufactory, situated in the Old Kent Road, London, was entirely consumed. The factory, which occupied an extensive space of ground, was built nearly all of wood; and, from the inflammable nature of the materials used in the business, there being upon the premises between 300 and 400 barrels of tar, pitch and resin, the whole was in one hour reduced to ashes.' When the Great Exhibition was held in 1851 at Hyde Park, the firm erected huge marquees and tents and decorated the interiors with flags and bunting. During the Second World War the company manufactured a variety of products including shrouds for civilian war dead and inflatable pontoons for salvage work. Many of the decoy tanks and transporters were constructed in the Edgington premises. A quarter-size model of their shop front can be seen in the courtyard of the Livesey Museum about a mile further along the old road leading out to Kent. The model shop front was presented to Southwark Council after the shop itself was removed in 1967 to make way for the Bricklayers Arms flyover. The original shop front can be seen at Woburn Abbey.

In 1904 Thursday was early closing day for Upton's.

South London was a leading centre for the silk and felt hat industry in the nineteenth century. One of the most important firms was started in 1869 by Frederick Upton who had premises at No. 68 London Road and Nos 2-4 St George's Road. From the outset the firm was conducted on enterprising and go-ahead lines. After the founder died in 1887, the work was continued by his son, L.J. Upton. He was brought up in the business and spent most of his life in it so he devoted practical and commercial experience to it. The firm's premises occupied a commanding position at the junction of Newington Causeway, Newington Butts, St George's Road, London Road and Walworth Road. They were entirely reconstructed in 1883 and were ornate. The ground floor was sub-divided into three main showrooms; two were occupied by the hat department and the other had hosiery and outfitting goods. A large retail business was conducted there in a variety of hats, caps, men's silk goods, hosiery and umbrellas. The whole of the upper floors, with the exception of several living rooms, were used either as stockrooms or for the wholesale trade, which extended to every part of the United Kingdom and also to many places abroad. The shipping branch was one of the notable features of the firm. It was well known that goods stamped with the name of 'Upton' met with a ready sale on the Colonial and American markets. At the rear of the building was the hat factory in which a large number of skilled people were employed in making hats and helmets. Among the specialities were the 'Bees'-wing' and 'Waynaut' silk and felt hats which were made exclusively by Upton's. The firm also made high-class felt hats for ladies and helmets for India and other hot countries.

Carty's, a firm that is known to have made vats and wooden tanks from at least 1766, occupied one of the oldest buildings in Peckham. The premises were at No. 2 Harders Road (now Woods Road), off Queens Road. In a book published by the Science Museum called *Vatmaking*, R.R. Foskett stated of Carty's: 'They were without doubt the foremost firm of vatmakers in Great Britain, with an unassailable reputation for the quality of their vessels and service'. It seems that the firm, which closed in 1989, originated in Borough High Street where it traded for over a century; although it was not known as Carty's throughout its history. In 1761 a lease was granted to Benjamin Powell and Edward Layton for building on a site previously occupied by buildings of the King's Bench Prison. The first mention of Powell & Layton trading as backmakers (an old term for vatmakers) is to be found in Kent's Directory for 1763, where their address is given as 'near St George's Church, Southwark'. The firm became Layton & Young in 1790. In St George the Martyr church are memorials to the family of Florance Young (that is, Florance with an 'a'; this was a man's name before Florence Nightingale popularized the name of the Italian city for women). Florance Young, who had an apprentice called Charles Carty, took over Layton & Young's. The firm became Carty, Son & Wingrove in 1845. In 1919 a newly formed company called Carty & Son Ltd was formed. The firm moved to Harders Road, Peckham, in 1921. In 1966 Carty's celebrated their bicentenary. Festivities included a dinner for the men and their wives at the Café Royal in Regent Street and the production of a commemorative booklet *1766-1966: 200 Years of Vatmaking*.

In 1983 Carty's was based in one of Peckham's oldest buildings.

In the 1920s Holdron's was a large department store in Peckham's Golden Mile.

Rye Lane was noted as one of South London's major shopping centres in the first half of the twentieth century. It was known as the Golden Mile. Its decline began in 1949 when Holdron's large store closed. Part of the firm's chimney, with RONS on it, can be seen in the Copeland Industrial Park. The firm began trading in around 1882 when Henry Holdron opened his 'Market' at No. 53 Rye Lane. Between 1885 and 1888 this had expanded to include existing shop premises on both sides, Nos 51-57. Similar development continued steadily until 1910. Holdron's had a special character but it was particularly susceptible to the economic difficulties of the 1920s and '30s. The pattern of trade was geared to meet these problems and encourage custom wherever possible. There were very long opening hours (9.00 a.m. until 7.00 p.m. on Monday, Tuesday and Wednesday; until 7.30 p.m. on Friday and 8.45 p.m. on Saturdays). There were frequent sale periods and special reductions. There was also a great deal of 'club' trading, which enabled the cost of a purchase to be spread over a period of time. During the Second World War there was a fire sub-station at Holdron's. Ironically, fire ripped through part of the former Holdron's store on 9 October 2001 when the Agora indoor market and Allied Carpets shop were destroyed. Local resident Doris Daniels recalls in *Peckham and Nunhead Remembered* (Tempus Publishing Ltd) working in Holdron's from the age of fourteen. She found it quite awe-inspiring as there were two long corridors leading to Rye Lane and there were commissionaires on the doors. Holdron's was acquired by the John Lewis Partnership in 1940; it was sold in 1949. Holdron's is also included in *The Story of Peckham and Nunhead* (Southwark Local Studies Library).

Howard Heinz, in the centre, was photographed with the staff at his Peckham factory in June 1922.

Heinz's first factory in England was in Peckham. The firm bought the old-established pickle manufacturers, Batty & Co. of No. 127 Brayards Road. The premises included a number of railway arches; seventeen were used for storage and two for processing bottled goods. Henry J. Heinz, the firm's founder, made his first sales call in England in 1886 but had no manufacturing facilities here until 1905 when Charles Hellen, a new manager from Boston in Massachusetts, purchased Batty's factory that was on the north side of Brayards Road between Caulfield Road and Stanbury Road. It was used until 1925 to produce the first Heinz products bottled in the United Kingdom. All canned goods were imported from the USA until the company moved to its new factory at Harlesden in 1925. The famous baked beans were not made here until 1928. Batty & Co. was established in 1824 and its name was kept on labels until 1910. Indeed, until the 1912 Kelly's Directory, 'W. Batty' appeared against the address at Brayards Road. From then until 1926 the listing was 'H.J. Heinz & W. Batty'. With the appearance of the Heinz name came their guarantee of a 'pure food product' and the assurance that 'your grocer will return the purchase price if it fails to please'. Howard Heinz was photographed with the staff of the Peckham factory in 1922. He took over the running of the family firm when his father died in 1919. The photograph was included in *100 Years of Progress*, a book published by the firm to celebrate its centenary, and in *Images of London: Peckham and Nunhead* (Tempus Publishing).

Cows were milked by hand, c. 1920.

London's last cow keeper kept his herd in Peckham until 1967. John Jorden, whose dairy was in Lugard Road, was a fourth-generation Peckham cow keeper. He kept in business against all odds with thirty to forty cows. John Jorden said in 1967: 'We were no longer competitive ... costs have been rising for all farmers in the last year or two. In our case when all feed has to be brought in from the country, they were crippling. Once we used to have our own dairy round, then we tried to cut costs and sell the milk to United Dairies. We could make no profit even from this. We got to the stage when we were just making enough to cover the debts.' Memories of the Peckham cows are included in *Peckham and Nunhead Remembered* (Tempus Publishing). Ray Byfield recalled being sent to the dairy for a bucket of manure 'at very little or no cost but it had to be retrieved yourself from a large smelly shed'. Myrtle Newman wrote: 'We enjoyed seeing the cows being milked. We knew their names – Daisy, Marigold and other names I have forgotten. The cows were there for a week and then taken to the country when a fresh lot would replace them. The milk was delicious.' On returning to Peckham after evacuation at Henley-on-Thames during the Second World War, Valerie Newman's family lived in Lugard Road and bought milk from the nearby dairy. John Jorden's dairy was not the only Peckham dairy that became well-known. Austin's of Peckham Rye, which was one of Europe's largest antique dealers, began as a dairy in Brayards Road. The story of that firm and an old picture of the dairy are in *Southwark Remembered* and a picture of John Jorden's dairy is in *Images of London: Peckham and Nunhead* (Tempus Publishing).

Crowds gathered outside Co-operative House on the day it opened.

Co-operative House, a landmark building in Peckham's Rye Lane, will be demolished soon but historical aspects of the façade will be incorporated in the new building on the site. The Royal Arsenal Co-operative Society, which began in 1868, opened a store at Nos 259-267 Rye Lane in 1913. This was remodelled and opened as Co-operative House on 12 October 1932. The architect was Mr T.W. Ackroyd, FRIBA. 'Crowds Throng Rye Lane Building' declared the *South London Press* in its report on the opening ceremony, which was witnessed by about 1,500 people. A huge crowd assembled in Rye Lane to hear the speeches through loudspeakers. The interior of the store was packed with visitors. Delegates numbering nearly 1,000 came from Co-operative organisations from all over south London. In his speech to the delegates, Mr E.J. Bale said: 'Some who are new in the movement may be wondering why so many people should gather to celebrate the opening of a new block of shops. The Co-operative Movement is more than the buying and selling of commodities. It is a weapon of the people for their own defence'. The new store was opened by Mr R.R. Wale, chairman of the Royal Arsenal Co-operative Society that employed 6,000 people. After inspecting the store, the Co-op delegates went in motor-coaches to Dulwich Baths for tea. In the evening they returned to Co-operative House for a concert in the grand hall. A ten-day celebration programme was arranged with concerts every night. Films and variety shows were held in the afternoons. Co-operative House, which closed in 1980, had nearly 1,800 electric lamps and ten miles of cables. Pictures of Co-operative House are included in *The Co-operative Way* by Ron Roffey.

In 1983 Roberts' Capsule Stopper factory provided employment in a pleasant environment overlooking Peckham Rye Common.

Roberts' Capsule Stopper factory overlooking Peckham Rye Common is likely to be demolished in the foreseeable future. This striking art deco building opened in 1931 and was designed by Wallis Gilbert and Partners who also designed the London Transport bus garage that opened in Peckham High Street in 1951. This was demolished in 1995-96 to make way for an extension to the Safeway store in the Aylesham Centre. Wallis Gilbert and Partners were also the architects of the Firestone factory in Brentford and the Hoover Building at Perivale. No one knows a great deal about the early days of Roberts' Capsule Stopper Co. Ltd, now Roberts' Metal Packaging Ltd. Messrs Roberts did not stay in the firm very long. However, the Post Office Trade Directories show that from the early 1880s there was a firm listed as Roberts & Son, Cork Merchants of No. 22 Harp Lane, Great Tower Street, EC. Sharing the same building and in the surrounding buildings were wine, tea and hide merchants. As Roberts had the raw material for making bottle stoppers, it is believed that a family member of the business decided to diversify and start a new line. In 1887, for the first time, Roberts Capsule Stopper Co. appeared alongside the familiar address of Roberts & Son Cork Merchants of No. 22 Harp Lane. Minutes of very early board meetings suggest that the two founders (believed to be brothers) were E.A. and F.C. Roberts. The new firm moved twice during its infancy before it found another factory in Canterbury Road, Peckham, in 1912. The new factory overlooking Peckham Rye was built on the site of Pineapple Lodge, home of market gardener Israel Solomon. Roberts' Capsule Stopper Co. Ltd is included in *Old Surviving Firms of South London* by Steven Harris.

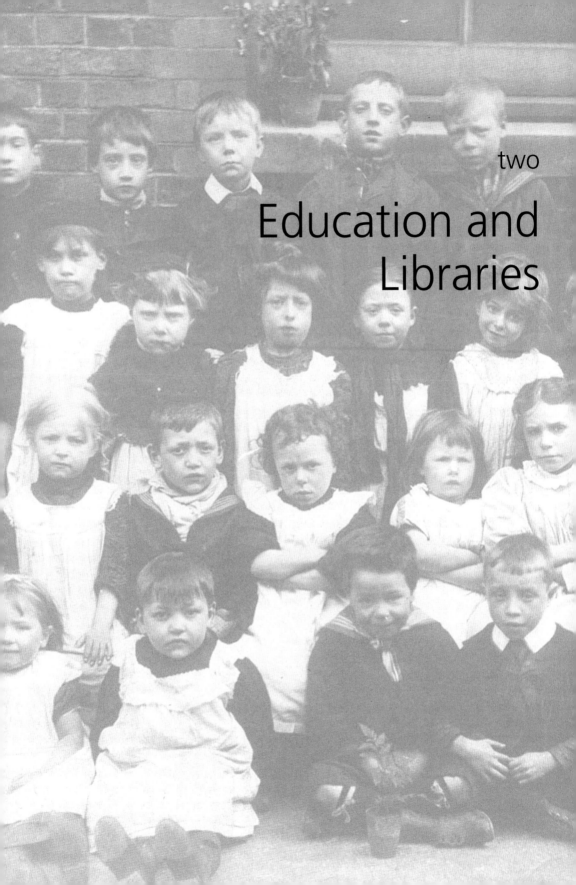

two

Education and Libraries

St Saviour's and St Olave's School for Girls in the New Kent Road owes its origin to the amalgamation of two ancient Foundations, St Olave's Grammar School and St Saviour's Grammar School for Boys. The two boys' schools had existed close to each other, with varying fortunes and in considerable rivalry, for over 300 years. Queen Elizabeth I granted a Royal Charter in 1562 to St Saviour's Grammar School, which was founded by the citizens of Southwark. In 1571 a similar charter was granted to St Olave's Grammar School and a new school was built in Tooley Street in 1892. Four years later St Olave's and St Saviour's schools were amalgamated. In 1899 there was a scheme to establish the St Saviour's and St Olave's Grammar School for Girls. In 1968 the boys in St Olave's Grammar School, Tooley Street, moved to a new school in Orpington. The present girls' school was opened in 1903 by their Royal Highnesses the Prince and Princess of Wales who in 1918, as King George V and Queen Mary, revisited the school. The school grew rapidly from 90 pupils in 1903 to nearly 400 by the end of the First World War. In 1928 a new wing was opened by HRH the Princess Royal. During the Second World War the school was evacuated, first to Hove and then Chertsey. Some damage was suffered by the building but the main structure stood firm despite being in an area that was devastated. To cope with additional pupils, the school was remodelled beginning in 1961. A new assembly hall, a well-equipped kitchen and four new science laboratories were added. The new building was opened by HRH Princess Alexandra in 1964. *Two Schools* by R.C. Carrington is an illustrated history of the two old schools.

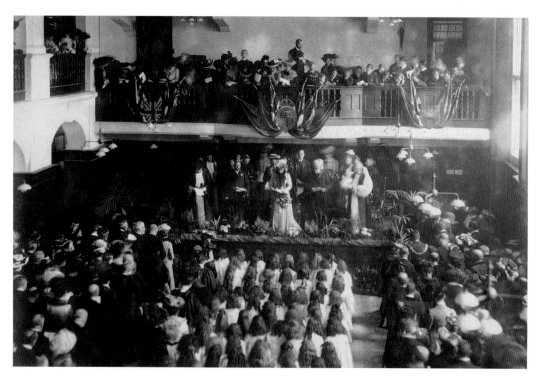

St Saviour's and St Olave's Grammar School for Girls was opened on 14 March 1903 by the Prince and Princess of Wales who became King George V and Queen Mary. Pupils from St Olave's and St Saviour's School for Boys are on the right in the gallery.

Grove Tavern was built on the site of Dr Glennie's Academy.

The Harvester at the Grove Tavern is on the site of Dr Glennie's Academy where Lord Byron (1788-1824) was a pupil for two years from 1799. His mother thought it advisable to move her son to London for the benefit of surgical advice. She was keen to place him in a quiet school where the means adopted for the cure of his lameness might be more easily attended to. As it was thought advisable for him to have a separate apartment to sleep in, Dr Glennie had a bed put up for him in his own study. During his stay in Dr Glennie's Academy, Byron was described as having been attentive to his studies, playful, good humoured and beloved by his companions. He was excessively fond of poetry and showed an extensive acquaintance with sacred history. Lord Byron's mother stayed close to the school and began to interfere. She wrote long notes to Dr Glennie about various aspects of education even though she was totally ignorant on the subject. She exasperated Dr Glennie by frequently reminding him that, because of his rank, her son deserved treatment quite different from that given to other boys. She even called in the middle of school hours and insisted loudly that her son be allowed out for the remainder of the day. Lord Byron was deeply ashamed of his mother. He had not wanted to go to the Dulwich school and resented Dr Glennie for insisting that he had to start studying Latin again from the beginning. In 1801 Byron was sent to Harrow. More information about Lord Byron, Dr Glennie's Academy and the Grove Tavern are included in *East Dulwich: An Illustrated Alphabetical Guide*.

A nondescript little building in Burchell Road, a side turning off Queen's Road in Peckham, has an interesting history. Previously called College Hall, it was attached to Peckham Collegiate School. This was originally known as Peckham School and was founded by the Revd Martin Ready in 1788. Adjoining his house opposite South Street (now Rye Lane), he built a chapel that he used on weekdays as a schoolroom. The school moved to Queen's Road in the second half of the nineteenth century. Some interesting people were pupils at the school. Dr Thomas Raffles (1788-1863) was an independent minister who achieved eminence in Liverpool and was chairman of the Congregational Union of England and Wales in 1839. Among his school friends was Richard Slate (1787-1867) who was minister of a Preston church for thirty-five years. He was the biographer of nonconformist minister Oliver Heywood (1630-1702) who was excommunicated in 1662 for not using the prayer book. Sir William Fry Channell (1804-73), who became a baron, was a pupil at Mr Ready's school by 1815 when his family were living in Hill Street (now Peckham Hill Street). He later became a judge. After Peckham Collegiate School closed, the hall behind the house at No. 80 Queen's Road was used by the brethren. College Hall was included in the census conducted by the *Daily News* and published in *The Religious Life of London* edited by Richard Mudie-Smith (published in 1904). This showed that thirty-five people attended in the morning of the survey and twenty-two in the evening. The former College Hall is now used by the Gospel Light Evangelical Ministry. The notable people who attended the Revd Martin Ready's school are included in *Who Was Who in Peckham* and College Hall has entries in *Peckham and Nunhead Churches*.

College Hall was photographed here, c. 1972.

The British and Foreign School Society's premises in Borough Road. The site is now used by London South Bank University.

Joseph Lancaster Primary School in Harper Road, SE1, commemorates an important educationist. Joseph Lancaster (1778-1838) was born in Kent Street, Southwark, and became a Quaker. In 1798 he opened his first school in Borough Road. As he did not have enough money to pay assistant teachers he used 'monitors', older boys and girls, to teach the younger ones. He claimed that in this way one master could manage 1,000 children. To save buying books they had pages of the Bible in large print hanging on the walls and children wrote on slates. The Duke of Bedford and Lord Somerville visited the school that Joseph Lancaster had founded and they became the friends and patrons of the system. Schools that followed the so-called 'Monitorial' system opened all over England and in other countries. Monitors went to Joseph Lancaster's school for training. In 1818 a black boy called William Jagon was monitor-general. He later became master of a school in the West Indies. Joseph Lancaster quarrelled with the committee of the Royal Lancasterian Institution (afterwards called the British and Foreign School Society), which was founded in 1808 to develop Joseph Lancaster's work. Ten years later he emigrated to America. He founded more than sixty schools in New York where he died. The British and Foreign Schools Society built a Teacher Training College in Borough Road. In 1890 the building was taken over by the Borough Polytechnic, which is now part of London South Bank University. Joseph Lancaster is included in *The Story of the Borough* by Mary Boast. This was published by Southwark Local Studies Library where other local history titles can be found including *Manual of the System of Primary Instruction pursued in the Model Schools of the British and Foreign School Society* (published in 1837), *A History of Borough Road College* by G.F. Bartle and *Teacher Extraordinary: Joseph Lancaster 1778-1838* by Mora Dickson.

Wilson's Grammar School was highly regarded when this photograph was taken, c. 1950.

Wilson's Annexe of Camberwell College of Arts uses the former Wilson's Grammar School that opened in 1882. It was designed by E.R. Robson, architect of the London School Board. Wilson's Grammar School was Camberwell's first known school. It was founded under Royal Charter in 1615 by Edward Wilson, Vicar of St Giles's, to give local boys, including twelve children of poor parents, such a knowledge of Latin and Greek as would enable them to go to a university and so enter either the clerical or one of the learned professions. The founder drew up 'fit and wholesome statutes' for the school; the choice of master took first place. He had to be 'sound in religion, body and mind; gentle, sober, honest, virtuous and discreet, and approved for a good facility in teaching'. A law suit brought against the governors by a Camberwell parishioner in 1843 went in favour of the governors, but the school had to pay the costs. As these were so high, the school had to close in 1845 and sell all its possessions apart from the land. For over thirty years the school remained closed but the governors and public-spirited citizens worked for its re-establishment. In 1880 Queen Victoria approved a new scheme for the administration of the old foundation. The school opened again in 1882 in new buildings close to the site of the old schoolhouse. Among the former pupils were Dr W.R. Matthews, Dean of St Paul's Cathedral; Sir Alan Cobham, aviation pioneer; Sir James Jeans, mathematician and astronomer; and R.S. Anderson, Dulwich Hamlet and England amateur international footballer. In 1975 Wilson's Grammar School moved to Sutton. The school is included in *The Story of Camberwell* by Mary Boast published by Southwark Local Studies Library.

In 1894 pupils at Orange Street School had the unusual experience of being photographed.

Jerwood Space in Union Street, SE1, uses the former Orange Street School that opened in 1874. The school is included in *Studies in Board Schools* by Charles Morley, which was published in 1897. 'Those whose fathers are out of work, hold up your hands', cried the master of Orange Street School; many hands were held up. It became John Harvard School in 1937 to commemorate the principal founder of Harvard College, Massachusetts, USA, John Harvard (1607-38) who left Southwark for North America in 1637. Orange Street was renamed Copperfield Street to celebrate the hero in Charles Dickens's novel *David Copperfield*. Some of the early part of the book was based on the author's own painful childhood experiences in that area. 'Of all my books, I like this the best', Dickens wrote, possibly because some of it was autobiographical. He added: '...like many fond parents I have in my heart of hearts a favourite child, and his name is David Copperfield'. After John Harvard School closed, the building became a Southwark Council training centre. In 1998 it was refurbished by the Jerwood Foundation to provide excellent and affordable rehearsal facilities for dance and theatre companies. The year-round programme in the Gallery (once the school's bike sheds) mainly features the art schemes and awards of the Jerwood Foundation. The former school also incorporates a popular café and the Glasshouse, which is used for various functions. Orange Street School and Jerwood Space are included in *The Story of Bankside* by Leonard Reilly and Geoff Marshall, which is available from Southwark Local Studies Library where *Studies in Board Schools* can be seen. Admission and discharge registers for Orange Street School and John Harvard School are held in the London Metropolitan Archives.

Blackfriars Road District Library, originally called Christ Church Library, was decorated for the coronation of George VI in 1937.

The small riverside parish of Christ Church showed commendable enterprise in 1889 by establishing a free public library in the Albert Institute. This was in a back street, Charles Street, in a badly-built edifice but it was highly appreciated. With much courage, industry and foresight the library commissioners then obtained two houses in Blackfriars Road, close to Nelson Square, and converted them into a library, which was opened on 18 June 1898 by Mr R.K. Causton, MP for West Southwark. He said that Christ Church was the only parish in London that had rented rooms for a public library. Mr Causton stated that the parish was situated in the poorest and most populous district of South London and that its inhabitants were compelled to live as closely as possible to their work. He said that the Library Commissioners were anxious to provide them with every opportunity for mental recreation. In the 1898 building there was a handsome reading room on the ground floor. Every part of the room was well lit from a large lantern or roof light in the centre. The reference library and lending library were also on the ground floor. There was a boardroom on the first floor for Christ Church Vestry. This ran local affairs until Christ Church became part of the Metropolitan Borough of Southwark in 1900. The people who crowded into the new building found that it was light, roomy, and admirably adapted for its purpose. Christ Church Library, which was totally destroyed during the Second World War, is shown on *Old Ordnance Survey Maps: Waterloo & Southwark 1914* (Godfrey Edition), which can be obtained from Southwark Local Studies Library which also holds press reports of the library opening.

Bermondsey Central Library was the most impressive building in Spa Road.

Local people in Bermondsey have pressurised Southwark Council to reopen Bermondsey Library, Spa Road, which closed in 1989. The impressive building was officially opened on Monday 18 January 1892 by Sir John Lubbock, MP who was a banker, scientist and author. He said that as time rolled on, the argument for libraries gained additional strength. The *South London Press* began its report of the opening by stating: 'Another public house in Bermondsey! – Sir John Lubbock's little pleasantry – will, at first blush, perhaps, be calculated to cause temperance reformers to open their eyes in wonder. But, stay! – the "public house" is not dedicated to the gratification of the palate, but of the mind, and is designed to further the all-important cause of education. In other words, Bermondsey's Public Library was formally opened by Sir John Lubbock on Monday.' The library was one of the most complete and best lighted in London. The principal entrance in the centre of the building, emphasised by an Ionic portico, led to a spacious hall and staircase. On the right was a newspaper reading room, which had over eighty English, Scottish and Irish newspapers. The lending library had shelves to take 20,000 books. The librarian's room and residence had a private entrance to the lending department. Stone stairs led to a first floor paved with marble mosaic. The reference library had a domical roof in the centre supported by four Corinthian columns. The foundation stone was laid by Mr A. Lafone, MP for Bermondsey. The architect was John Johnson; his design was selected out of fifty-seven submitted in public competition. The site cost £3,000 and the building cost £7,000. The former Bermondsey Library is included in *A Bermondsey and Rotherhithe Album* and *Bermondsey and Rotherhithe Perceived* by Peter Marcan.

Camberwell Central Library occupied the site in Peckham Road where Kingfisher House is today between the Pharoahs pub (destroyed by fire on 9 July 2004) and Pelican House. It was bombed during the Second World War. The library was opened on 9 October 1893 by HRH the Prince of Wales who became Edward VII after his mother, Queen Victoria, died. The Prince, accompanied by the Duke and Duchess of York, went to the new library after opening the South London Fine Art Gallery a short distance away in the same road. A guard of honour of the First Surrey Rifle Volunteers was posted at the entrance. The royal guests were greeted at the library by the Lord Mayor of the City of London, Alderman Sir Stuart Knill, who was born in Camberwell. They were taken by the architect and builder through the library and then into the pretty recreation ground at the rear of the building. The Prince made a speech in which he wished, 'the success of this fine new building, so well arranged, so complete, so well built in every respect'. Mr Frederick G. Banbury, MP for Peckham, said that he did not think anyone would deny that education conferred innumerable advantages upon a nation or that public libraries were important in disseminating knowledge among all classes of the community. The library was built in Jacobean Renaissance style. The architect was Robert Whellock who designed three buildings in SE15 that still exist – the Livesey Museum, Nunhead Library and the former Central Hall in Peckham High Street. The new library replaced a temporary central library in the High Street, Peckham. Camberwell Central Library is among over 200 pictures included in *Images of London: Peckham and Nunhead* (Tempus Publishing). The programme for the library opening can be seen in Southwark Local Studies Library.

Camberwell Central Library was featured on this postcard, c. 1905.

Newington Library, seen here around 1930, was prominent in Walworth Road.

Newington Library in Walworth Road has a stone inside the entrance saying that it was opened on 28 November 1893 by HRH Helena, Princess of Great Britain and Ireland, who was also Princess Christian of Schleswig-Holstein. She was the third daughter of Queen Victoria and was renowned for her philanthropic work with regard to hospitals and other charitable institutions. The official opening was a great occasion with a guard of honour provided by the Queen's Royal West Surrey Regiment. Upstairs in the Reference Library Her Royal Highness declared: 'I have much pleasure in declaring this library now open for public use'. The Bishop of Rochester moved a vote of thanks to Princess Christian and in his speech stated: 'To properly equip our young men and women for the battle of life, education must be commenced in the school and completed in the library'. The dignitaries assembled in the library cheered this comment. When Princess Christian and her daughter, Princess Aribert of Anhalt, left the library they were met with a very enthusiastic reception from the enormous number of spectators who made it difficult for the tramcars to get along the road outside the new library. During the evening about 10,000 people passed through the building and 300 copies of the library catalogue were sold. About 4,000 applications were made for borrowers' forms. In April 1895 the reference department was opened with 1,200 books. Within four years of opening, the library had nearly 20,000 books. The building cost £11,000 and the site £4,750. In *The Story of Walworth* Mary Boast wrote that 'it was only after a public campaign, with speakers using a wagon in Rodney Road as an open air platform, that local ratepayers were convinced of Newington's need for a library'.

The Reading Room of Southwark Bridge Road District Library, originally St Saviour's Library, is seen here in 1921.

The former St Saviour's Library in Southwark Bridge Road will become a cultural and creative industries training centre in the foreseeable future. The inscription on the foundation stone states that it was laid on 31 July 1893 by Richard Knight Causton, MP. The *South London Press* reported on Saturday 5 August that a copy of the paper and *The Times* were deposited in a cavity under the building together with a list of subscribers, a copy of the day's proceedings and *Free Public Libraries, their organisation, uses and management* by T. Greenwood (1887). A drawing accompanied the *South London Press*'s report of the opening of the library that took place on 2 November 1894 – a few months after Tower Bridge was opened. The Prince of Wales was due to perform the opening ceremony but because the Czar of Russia (Alexander III) died the previous day, the Prince (who became Edward VII) had to make a long and arduous journey to the Crimea for the funeral. The *South London Press* reported that 'the streets were gay with bunting, and there was a general air of enthusiasm over the opening'.

The local newspaper said: 'Great care had been taken in the selection of books, and the committee hoped they would be found extremely useful and instructive to the lower classes of St Saviour's.' The library was opened by Richard Causton, MP for Southwark, who said it would make the lives of the poor people happier. Southwark was a very densely populated area and about 63 per cent were poor. Behind the palatial warehouses lived many poor people who paid high rents and had few comforts. The library marked another step in Southwark's progress; it would soon possess public baths, the MP said, and it already had a fine polytechnic. The library closed in 1977 and was replaced by the John Harvard Library.

George Orwell wrote in St Olave's Library, seen here in 1933.

Novelist George Orwell wrote his Hop-Picking Diary in St Olave's Library that stood at the corner of Tooley Street and Potters' Fields in Bermondsey. Towards the end of the diary and before his notes he wrote: 'Most of this narrative was written in the Bermondsey public library, which has a good reading room and was convenient for the lodging house'; the lodging house was Lew Levy's kip in Tooley Street. St Olave's Library was opened on 7 April 1902 in the St Olave and St John's Institute. This building, which belonged to the United Charities of St Olave and St John, had been opened by HRH the Duke of Cambridge on 28 November 1898. The building had three floors. The basement was originally intended for a gymnasium and the ground floor as a library, billiard room and caretaker's apartments. The library had not been a success so local residents agitated for a public library to be established. The St Olave's Library should have been opened by the Mayor of Bermondsey, Colonel Bevington, but his leg was injured when he was thrown out of a cab. The opening ceremony was therefore performed by Cllr Henry Vezey who was vice-chairman of the Public Libraries Committee. The new library had 8,000 volumes; 500 had been left by the trustees of the United Charities of St Olave and St John. A large number of daily and weekly newspapers were provided in the news-rooms. A report of the library's opening was published in the *Southwark and Bermondsey Recorder* on 12 April 1902. This can be seen on microfilm in Southwark Local Studies Library. A picture of Colonel Bevington's statue in Tooley Street is included in *Bermondsey and Rotherhithe Perceived* by Peter Marcan. St Olave's Library closed in 1970.

Left: *Old Kent Road District Library was decorated for the coronation of George VI in 1937.*

Opposite: *Councillor Miss Rosina Whyatt was the Mayor of Camberwell when Peckham Hill Street Library was opened in 1954.*

The Old Kent Road Library, which was the most architecturally distinguished library in the London Borough of Southwark, was demolished in 1968 to make way for the Bricklayers Arms flyover. The foundation stone was laid on 8 March 1907 by HRH Princess Christian, third daughter of Queen Victoria. The library was opened by Lady Llangattock on 30 January 1908 at the junction of the Old and New Kent Roads. The site was given by Lord Llangattock and his son, the Hon. John Maclean Rolls. Andrew Carnegie, British-born United States industrialist and philanthropist, contributed £7,000 towards the cost of the building. The architect was Claude Batley. The building was in the late perpendicular Gothic style using Portland stone with Westmorland slates for the roof. The principal feature was the clock tower carrying as a weather vane a representation of a Viking ship. This alluded to the siege of London by King Canute (Cnut) when he brought ships up a canal, which he allegedly dug in the vicinity of the site, to allow his ships to pass London Bridge. A Chaucer window in the library showed the Canterbury pilgrims starting from the Tabard Inn, which also stood near the site. Other leaded windows commemorated Sir John Falstaff, a local worthy of the fifteenth century, John Gower (whose tomb is in Southwark Cathedral), Oliver Goldsmith, Charles Dickens, Eliza Cook, Coventry Patmore, John Ruskin, John Harvard and Andrew Carnegie. In his speech at the opening ceremony, the Revd W.J. Sommerville (chairman of the library committee) said he hoped the library would not be the home for loafers but be of real benefit to the residents. This was applauded. The picture above is one of many photographs included in *Southwark: The Twentieth Century* by Stephen Humphrey.

The award winning Peckham Library replaced the Peckham Hill Street Library where flats will probably be built. The old library was opened on 20 March 1954 and it was built because the Camberwell Central Library in Peckham Road was bombed in the Second World War. Due to the difficult economic situation in 1952, the Minister of Local Government cancelled Camberwell Council's plans to build a new prefabricated library in Peckham Hill Street. The new library had been approved in principle by the Minister the previous year and tenders for the work had been obtained by the council. A site was leased from the London County Council. As a result of the review of the capital investment programme for 1952, the amount allocated for miscellaneous local government services was greatly reduced. There were increased restrictions on all local authority civil building works, except housing, and so the new library had to be deferred until the economic situation improved. Two years later the library was opened by the Mayor of Camberwell, Cllr Rosina Whyatt. It was Camberwell's tenth public library and was nicknamed 'The Rainbow Library' by the mayor who commented on the colourful layout of the prefab building: 'It may not look much from the outside – you cannot do much with the exterior of a prefab, but it is a revelation to come inside', said the mayor. A mural was painted on the outside of the library in 1996 by East Dulwich artist Stan Peskett. The new Peckham library was opened in 2000.

Mary Boast, seen here in 1978, was Southwark's first Local Studies Librarian. The Southwark Room was in Newington Library.

Southwark Local Studies Library opened in 1978 at No. 211 Borough High Street, which is close to Borough Underground Station and at the rear of John Harvard Library. It superseded the Southwark Room at Newington Library in Walworth Road. This had dated from 1967 and was becoming increasingly cramped. The collections in the Southwark Room were brought together from various places in what had been the three separate boroughs of Bermondsey, Camberwell and Southwark until 1965. These collections had been partly inherited from predecessors of the borough councils from as far back as Tudor times. They had partly been accumulated after local public libraries had first been opened in the late 1880s. Mary Boast was appointed as the first Local Studies Librarian in 1972. Previous to that she had been an active local historian for many years. In her days in the Camberwell Public Libraries (from 1954) she followed the well-known borough librarian, the late William Hahn, in giving lectures on local history. Later she won much praise for her enterprising series of Neighbourhood Histories and for her many contributions to exhibitions at the South London Art Gallery. In 1994 Mary Boast was awarded the Freedom of the Borough, a remarkable civic honour. Mary happily continues to write and lecture even though she is now in her eighties.

three

Housing

The Drapers' Company built almshouses in Hill Street (now Glasshill Street, SE1).

Former old almshouses can be seen in Glasshill Street, SE1. They were opened by the Drapers' Company in 1820. The story of them begins with John Walter, who was born in Hereford and became a citizen of London. At first he was a Girdler (a maker of girdles) but he was appointed Clerk to the Drapers' Company in 1616 and held the clerkship for forty years. On his retirement in 1656 he was elected on to the Court of Assistants. This was a very unusual honour but was no doubt in recognition of his benefactions and long service as clerk. During his lifetime John Walter resolved to found almshouses because many poor people 'had lately perished by lying abroad in the cold for want of habitation, to the great dishonour of God'. He communicated his intentions to some friends who induced parishioners of St George, Southwark, to provide a site. By 1650 almshouses had been erected. John Walter expressed a wish to remain anonymous until after his death. By his will he left property in trust for the maintenance of the alms folk. New almshouses, now known as St George's Cottages, were built on a different site in what today is Glasshill Street. They consisted of a row of five houses of two storeys, which in total housed sixteen occupants. In front of the houses were gardens and behind was a long row of fuel stores and washhouses. In 1961 the Drapers' Company built new almshouses called Walter's Close, in Brandon Street, to replace old ones in Draper Street. A decade later they enlarged them to house the residents from Glasshill Street. An 1851 drawing of Drapers' Almshouses is included in *Southwark Past* by Richard Tames. Information is in *Survey of London: St George's Fields* (London County Council, 1955) and *The Story of Bankside* by Leonard Reilly and Geoff Marshall.

The Elizabeth Baxter Hostel was looking careworn in 1977.

The Oasis Trust uses the Elizabeth Baxter Hostel at No. 52 Lambeth Road as a Health Centre for homeless people. It is a Grade II listed building that has been used to help needy people for over 150 years. The *Gentleman's Magazine* (July 1841) reported: 'May 28. The first stone was laid of the new building of the Royal South London Dispensary. The increase of population in Lambeth and the vicinity has induced the trustees of this institution to commence the erection of a suitable building, on an enlarged scale, on the space opposite Bethlem Hospital. The ceremony was performed by his Royal Highness the Duke of Cambridge, Vice-Patron of the charity, assisted by the Lord Bishop of Winchester. The architect is Mr. Sydney Smirke.' He designed the portico and dome of nearby Bedlam and the domed Reading Room of the British Museum. The Royal South London Dispensary had been established in 1821 to provide medical aid to poor sick people in the parishes of Lambeth and north Southwark. The hostel was founded in 1906 for the welfare of girls and women at risk. It became the Elizabeth Baxter Hostel in 1927 to commemorate the wife of the Revd M.P. Baxter. They were founders of *The Christian Herald*. In addition, Mr Baxter gave tickets to people in desperate need so they could obtain free food or a bed for the night. The hostel is mentioned in *Survey of London Volume XXV St George's Fields* (published by the London County Council). This can be seen in Southwark Local Studies Library as can annual reports and various papers (1845-1900) relating to the Royal South London Dispensary.

London Park Hotel at the Elephant & Castle opened in 1972 but was originally a Rowton House having 805 cubicles for working men. It was the third in a series of 'Poor Man's Hotels' started by Montagu William Lowry Corry, Lord Rowton (1838-1903). He had been private secretary to Benjamin Disraeli and Sir Edward Guinness asked him to be a trustee of the Guinness Trust in 1889. Lord Rowton made a survey of London's common lodging houses for the Trust and decided to establish working men's hotels. The Rowton House at Newington Butts opened on 23 December 1897. The best possible lodgings were provided for the small charge of 6d per night. The *South London Press* reported the opening by saying: 'The bill of fare would not have shamed a high-class restaurant. A large plate of turkey was to be had for eightpence; roast beef, sixpence; leg of pork and apple sauce, fourpence; vegetables, one penny; and plum pudding, mince pies, rice, and "college" [small plum pudding], one penny.' The reading room contained a large variety of engravings representing scenes from Shakespeare. The smoking room was also decorated with engravings and stags' heads. All the residents seemed comfortable, and several of the older lodgers acknowledged that Rowton House was the best and cleanest place they had dossed in since they left their homes. Only men were accommodated. The women bed-makers entered the building only when the lodgers had left their cubicles and an iron dividing gate had been shut. In building the new house 1,650,000 bricks were used, 200 tons of steel joists, 1,500 tons of Portland cement and 1,700 tons of cork breeze. There were three miles of piping and two-and-a-half acres of flooring and paving. The house overlooked a beautiful open space – the disused churchyard of St Mary, Newington.

Right: *The author of* King Solomon's Mines, *H. Rider Haggard, wrote about the Bermondsey Salvation Army centre.*

Opposite: *London Park Hotel used to be a Rowton House.*

Spa Home, a social service centre owned and managed by the Salvation Army in Spa Road, Bermondsey, was demolished in 2003. Known originally as the Spa Road Elevator, it was opened in 1899. In the same year the Salvation Army launched a £50,000 Century Appeal to develop social services throughout the country. It was reported that, '150 men are employed at Spa Road, and paper and rag sorting will be the principal industries, with a home for the men employed'. Sir Henry Rider Haggard reported on the Spa Road Elevator in his 1910 book *Regeneration*. The following year General William Booth formally opened an extension to the Elevator. In 1913 a serious fire occurred in the paper-sorting wing, which caused much damage. During the First World War refugees from Belgium were sheltered at the Spa Road centre. In 1917 a Salvage Unit was established dealing with furniture and used clothing. Men were sent out with handcarts to collect donations. These were eventually replaced with lorries and a petrol pump and tank were built into a corner of the site. The complex was expanded in 1925 by the addition of a tin box factory and also a direct access hostel for homeless men. During the Second World War Brigadier Arthur Micklethwaite, manager of the Spa Road centre, was killed by enemy bombing while working for the people in the local community. In 1971 the Spa Road Complex was established. The amalgamation brought together under one management the direct access hostel, the family service centre providing furniture and clothing to needy people, the laundry, and the rehabilitation workshop programme that had been established earlier. By 2002, after 103 years, the Spa Road Social Service Centre equalled the longest running use of one site by the Salvation Army for a Men's Social Centre.

The first estate erected by Camberwell Borough Council, the Grove Vale Estate, is one hundred years old. Plaques on Nos 106 and 129B Copleston Road give details of the estate that was built between 1903 and 1905. The houses were erected on land that had been part of Plagquett Hall Farm. Information about the estate's history is included in the Council's Annual Reports which can be seen in Southwark Local Studies Library. The 1902/03 edition stated: 'By the improvement a detour of over half a mile is saved in travelling from Peckham to East Dulwich, and an increasing volume of traffic pouring through the new roads proves the general value of the scheme'. Before new roads were made, Copleston Road, Bellenden Road and Oglander Road were culs-de-sac, as was what today is Everthorpe Road. Oxenford Street was a completely new road. This was named after the playwright John Oxenford who was born in Camberwell. The foundation stone of the new estate was laid by the Mayor of Camberwell, Cllr Goddard Clarke, on 27 May 1903. The stone bore the inscription: 'This estate is the property of the Borough of Camberwell, and the 85 houses thereon are the first buildings erected by the Council under the Housing of the Working Classes Act'. This 1890 Act had resulted from the Royal Commission on Housing set up in 1884. That highlighted the need to eradicate slums. As private landlords were largely concerned with making profit, councils became responsible for providing decent homes. The London County Council provided the money for Camberwell Borough Council to build this estate on two meadows. Pictures of the Grove Vale Estate are included in *Images of London: Peckham and Nunhead* (Tempus Publishing) and *The Story of Peckham and Nunhead* (Southwark Local Studies Library).

Right: *Ada Lewis House is seen here in 1960 before it became Driscoll House Hotel.*

Opposite: *The new Oxenford Street was photographed on 26 September 1904.*

Driscoll House Hotel, a prominent feature in the New Kent Road, was opened as Ada Lewis Home on 28 January 1913. This lodging house for 240 women was opened by Princess Louise (Duchess of Argyll). The chairman of the board of trustees, Mr E.H. Davies, explained how the building came to be erected. Some years earlier their deputy chairman, Sir Algernon West, wrote to Mrs Ada Lewis asking whether she would provide £40,000 for the purpose of building houses for working-class women. As he did not receive a reply, he assumed that his letter had been put in a waste paper basket. However, after Mrs Lewis had died it was found that she had left £50,000 and other endowments for a Home for Women on the Rowton House principle. The trustees were appointed by the Court of Chancery and the home they had built in memory of Ada Lewis was of 'a very superior nature, and might really be termed an hotel rather than a lodging-house', as the *Southwark and Bermondsey Recorder* described it in a report of the opening. The *South London Press* on 31 January 1913 published a lengthy report giving the names of all the guests at the opening ceremony. For sixpence a night or 3s a week a poor woman could have a bedroom (not a cubicle). There were a few larger rooms for mothers and daughters or sisters, containing two beds, at 10d for the night or 5s for the week. More than 50,000 guests from 210 countries have stayed in the building during the last 91 years. Driscoll House Hotel at No. 172 New Kent Road, SE1 has 200 rooms. Additional information about the Ada Lewis Home can be found in Southwark Local Studies Library.

The Mayor of Camberwell addressed the invited guests at the official opening of the Acorn Estate in 1963.

An invited guest stormed off the platform at the opening of the Acorn Estate in Queens Road, Peckham. The headline on the front page lead story in the *South London Press* on 23 July 1963 was: TORY CANDIDATE WALKS OUT ON GEORGE BROWN. The Dulwich Tory candidate, Martin Stevens, left the platform at the opening of Camberwell Borough Council's Acorn Estate the previous Saturday after what he called 'unforgivable statements' by George Brown, Deputy Leader of the Labour Party. Mr Stevens, who was a Camberwell councillor, wrote immediately to the Mayor, Cllr Harry Lamborn (who became MP for Southwark in 1972 and Peckham from 1974 until his death in 1982): 'You must have been embarrassed as I was to witness this tasteless tantrum on the part of the Deputy Leader of the Labour Party. As a representative of the Conservative group of the council I had no choice but to leave the platform'. Mr Brown spoke about the Profumo and Rachman affairs and said: 'Now the truth is out we must stop attention wandering off on the sordid byways of the seamy side of life and get an understanding of the basic requirements for a housing policy. First the Rent Act must go. We must replace it with legislation for the needs of the tenant. The tenant cannot look after himself. It is now crystal clear that housing by its very nature must be treated as a social service'. Photographs of the opening of the Acorn Estate are included in *Images of London: Peckham and Nunhead* (published by Tempus Publishing).

four

Organisations

Charterhouse Mission built St Hugh's, Crosby Row, in 1898. This photograph shows the building being extended to house a gym and a working men's club in the early years of the twentieth century.

Charterhouse-in-Southwark has been helping people and the community for over a century. But the story really began much further back in history. In the City of London in 1123 the priory and hospital of St Bartholomew was founded at Smithfield. Thirteen acres of the land were bought in 1349 by the gallant knight Sir Walter Manny as a burial place for 50,000 victims of the Black Death. Here in 1370 he established a monastery of the Carthusian order. A house, later built on the site, was bought in 1611 by Thomas Sutton, 'esteemed the richest commoner in England', for his 'Hospital of King James, founded in Charterhouse in the County of Middlesex'. It was to educate forty-four boys and provide lodging for eighty poor gentlemen. The school moved to a healthier site outside London, in the Surrey countryside at Godalming, in 1872. It was decided in the next decade 'that Charterhouse should follow the example of ... other great Schools, by establishing a mission in some of the crowded lanes and alleys of London'. The idea was evidently particularly appealing to Dr Haig Brown, the headmaster, who had brought the school out of the smoke and stench of Clerkenwell to Godalming. Why Southwark was chosen for a mission is not known. In 1885 the Revd J.G. Curry was appointed as the first missioner and established Charterhouse-in-Southwark on the first of its present three sites. By July 1885 it was operating in two rooms of a small building, No. 40 Tabard Street, 'a newly built shop'. *Charterhouse-in-Southwark* by Shirley Corke tells the story, illustrated with photographs, from then until 2000. It can be obtained from the organisation at No. 40 Tabard Street, SE1 4JU.

Pelican House was a prominent feature in Peckham Road in 1979.

The former Pelican House in Peckham Road, which was renamed Winnie Mandela House in 1989, will be demolished and replaced with housing in the foreseeable future. The pelicans on the present building are a reminder that Pelican House School occupied the site in the nineteenth century. When W.H. Blanch wrote *Ye Parish of Camerwell* (published in 1875) the building was at least 200 years old. The pelicans, from which the name was derived, originally stood on brick pilasters at the entrance gates. The school used the former home of Miles Stringer, who took an active part in all local affairs. The Surrey Association for the General Welfare of the Blind, which was established in 1857, had premises in Peckham Road that can be traced back as far as 1880. In 1910 the organisation became the London Association for the Blind and is now Action for Blind People. In 1924 power machinery was installed to manufacture knitting needles and bangles. This was the first time a visually impaired person had operated power machinery anywhere. The workshop premises were extended in 1928/29. As the Post Office placed orders for a new type of basket in 1936, work began on extending the premises again. New offices at Pelican House were completed in 1952/53. HRH Princess Alexandra of Kent toured the workshops and offices in 1961. The factory departments moved to Verney Road, Bermondsey, in 1974 and Pelican House was sold two years later. The basket used in the film *Around the World in Eighty Days* was made at Pelican House.

A 1979 view of Camberwell New Road shows a flower shop where the Camberwell Provident Dispensary was based in the nineteenth century.

An old shop with tall chimneys in Camberwell New Road has a plaque stating:

FOUNDED 1862. REBUILT BY VOLUNTARY CONTRIBUTIONS 1880.
CHARLES DRUCE PRESIDENT. OTTO A. BENECKE TREASURER

The building belonged to the Camberwell Provident Dispensary, which was established for the purpose of assisting poor people within a radius of one-and-quarter miles of St Giles's church; and was an organisation that encouraged the habits of forethought and independence. The members, whose earnings could not exceed 30s a week, paid between 2d and 8d a month. When they were ill they received medical attention and medicine. There were more than 6,000 members in the 1870s. About 7,000 visits were made every year to poor people in their homes and about 14,000 consultations were held annually at the dispensary. During 1873, 156 married women were attended in their confinement and about 320 operations were performed by the dentist, Mr Thomson of Denmark Hill. The organisation's treasurer, Otto Benecke, lived in a house where Ruskin Park is today; its site is marked by a small pedestal which was once a sundial. The composer Felix Mendelssohn visited the home of the Benecke family who were related to his wife. There he composed the *Spring Song* which was originally entitled *Camberwell Green*. W.H. Blanch wrote about the Camberwell Provident Dispensary in *Ye Parish of Camerwell*. This was published in 1875 and is an invaluable reference book on Camberwell's history. It can be seen in Southwark Local Studies Library. The Minet Library has an expanded edition of the book which includes lots of items collected by W.F. Noble. These include a leaflet published by the Camberwell Provident Dispensary, which states: 'This prompt and timely aid afforded by the Dispensary is not only effectual for the cure of disease, but often for arresting it in its early stages'.

When the former Albert Institute was photographed in 1977, it was the headquarters of the Electoral Reform Society.

The Electoral Reform Society has been based in Chancel Street SE1 (originally Robert Street) since 1968. The building was first opened as the Albert Institute in 1887. The basement contained a washhouse, laundry, baths, kitchen and a lavatory for men. On the right-hand side of the building were five sets of rooms (comprising a living room, bedroom and scullery). The upper storey was a dormitory for single men. The institute started in Gravel Lane and the stone-laying ceremony for the original Albert Institute was performed by Lord Ashley who became the Earl of Shaftesbury; Eros in Piccadilly Circus commemorates him. The institute's first building was opened in August 1859 by Lord Radstock, who read an address in the name of the inhabitants of Christ Church parish. He expressed thanks to the Lord Mayor for consenting to inaugurate the institution and announced that HRH the Prince Consort, husband of Queen Victoria, had consented to be patron of the institute – hence the name. The institute was established by a rector of Christ Church, Blackfriars Road, the Revd Joseph Brown, to provide baths, meeting and club rooms, living rooms for married couples, and a dormitory for single men. Before the institute was built, washing-day was a dreaded event and a bath an almost unheard-of luxury. The original Albert Institute was acquired in 1872 by the South Eastern Railway Co. and demolished three years later. Drawings of both buildings used by the Albert Institute are included in *Sketches of Southwark – Old and New* by Robert Woodger Bowers and the later building is shown in *Visions of Southwark* by Peter Marcan.

Left: *This was the entrance to the Blackfriars Settlement when it was based in Nelson Square.*

Opposite: *HM Queen Elizabeth, who became the Queen Mother, visited the Time & Talents centre with Queen Juliana of the Netherlands in 1950. They were accompanied by the Mayor of Bermondsey, Cllr Eileen Greenwood.*

Blackfriars Settlement, which does vital work for people and the community, left Nelson Square in 2001, having been based there for over a century. It began as the Women's University Settlement and was set up by women's colleges in London, Cambridge and Oxford. In 1887 the Cambridge Ladies' Discussion Society invited the wife of the Revd Samuel Barnett, founder of Britain's first Settlement at Toynbee Hall in Stepney, to speak about the Settlement idea. At this meeting Miss Alice Grüner, a former student of Newnham College, spoke of her experiences as she worked from No. 44 Nelson Square in Southwark. According to Charles Booth's survey, this was the second poorest area of London after Bethnal Green. Soon a committee was formed with representatives from the Cambridge colleges of Newnham and Girton and the Oxford colleges of Lady Margaret Hall and Somerville, and the first women's settlement was established. The Women's University Settlement (WUS) worked from Miss Grüner's base. Its first paid warden was Helen Gladstone, the daughter of Prime Minister William Ewart Gladstone. A letter from philanthropist Octavia Hill described the pioneers of the Settlement by saying: 'They are all very refined, highly cultivated ... and very young. And they are so sweet and humble and keen to learn about the things out of their old line of experience'. The first volume of the Minute Books records a meeting on 27 June 1887 of the Executive Committee of the Women's University Settlement. Its objective was to 'promote the welfare of the poorer districts of London, more especially of the women and children, by devising and advancing schemes which tend to elevate them, and by giving them additional opportunities for education and recreation'. WUS changed its name to Blackfriars Settlement in 1961. *Blackfriars Settlement: a short history 1887-1987* is available free from the Blackfriars Settlement, 1-5 Rushworth Street, SE1 0RB.

The organisation Time & Talents, based in the Old Mortuary near the entrance to Rotherhithe Tunnel, has been involved in community development and social action since 1887. It originated in the drawing rooms of Victorian society and was started by a group of Christian women who inspired others into charitable work. Time & Talents centres began spreading all over England, Scotland, Ireland and abroad and after two years the membership stood at over 1,100. In 1898 a house in Bermondsey Square was used as the first base for Time & Talents activities in Bermondsey. The rich and comfortable young ladies had been totally unaware that people in Bermondsey lived in such poverty. The ladies held Bible classes and visited factories at lunch time to talk, sing and distribute flowers, which many had never seen before. The main object of their work was to help thousands of factory girls in Bermondsey. They therefore worked hard to raise money for the new Settlement at No. 187 Bermondsey Street that opened in 1908; the building still exists. The Time & Talents workers drew the attention of factory owners to the large number of accidents that happened; this contributed to various reforms to working conditions. They worked hard to provide holidays in the country for the factory workers and their children. In 1913 a hostel was developed to house factory girls who experienced severe overcrowding at home. Time & Talents fell on hard times during the 1960s. All its properties were sold. Clubs for older isolated people were run from a small flat in Bermondsey. Since the 1980s the Old Mortuary has developed as an important community centre. *By Peaceful Means: The Story of Time and Talents 1887-1987* by Marjorie Daunt can be obtained from Time & Talents Association, The Old Mortuary, St Marychurch Street, SE16 4JE.

A nightclub at No. 43 Peckham High Street uses a building which opened as the Central Hall of the People's League on Sunday 11 November 1894. The *South London Press* reported the opening and described the hall as, 'a well-lighted, handsome structure, provided with a gallery and capable of accommodating 1,000 persons'. The architect was Robert P. Whellock who also designed Nunhead Library and what today is the Livesey Museum. The People's League, of which John Robert Lees was President, had comprehensive and practical objectives. Its propaganda belonged to the realm of socialism – 'this word being used in its liberal, broad and unsectarian sense'. It aimed at realizing and applying religion of a practical, Christian, undenominational kind based on brotherhood. In his address at the opening ceremony, John Lees said that the hall was not a Baptist Chapel but as far as he could make it, it would be a house of God dedicated to humanity. This received cheers from the audience. In the evening the hall was packed and a large number of people were unable to obtain admission. The Central Hall was used by Baptists in 1900. After they moved out in 1908, the Revd G. Ernest Thorn founded the Church of the Strangers there and remained as minister until 1932. He dressed in a suit of armour when preaching on 'Put on the whole armour of God' and dressed as a rich young ruler to illustrate another Bible message. The Central Hall, which was sold in 1935, is included in *Peckham and Nunhead Churches*, and Ernest Thorn is among over 125 people in *Who Was Who In Peckham*.

Left: *The Central Hall was sold in 1935.*

Opposite: *Queen Mary travelled along Friary Road on her way to open the Union of Girls' Schools for Social Service in 1931.*

Princess Margaret paid many visits to The Peckham Settlement, which is sited on the corner of Staffordshire Street and Goldsmith Road. The main part of the premises is a former Wesleyan Chapel that was opened in 1834. This was purchased in 1929 on behalf of the Union of Girls' Schools for Social Service, which was originally founded in 1896 and supported by girls' schools around Britain. Queen Mary opened the present building in 1931. It was renamed The Peckham Settlement in 1992. Princess Margaret was its patron from 1947 until 2002. She wrote the foreword to *The Peckham Settlement 1896-2000* by Jennifer Stephens which is packed with pictures illustrating the fascinating history of this important organisation. Princess Margaret wrote: 'My Grandmother, Queen Mary, was especially interested in the Peckham area of London... During many years of Patronage, I have followed the settlement's progress with great interest, and have been present on many occasions, both to meet those closely involved and to celebrate landmarks in its history. The settlement represents a fine example of pioneering and dedicated voluntary work. The way in which it has adapted to the modern world and contributed to the very different and complex problems that need to be solved is to be admired and applauded'. The Peckham Settlement is committed to raising money to build new premises for existing and new services particularly focused on children and young people. New premises will give a vital boost to the organisation's invaluable work with individuals and in the community.

Peckham Lodge, formerly the headquarters of the Amalgamated Union of Engineering Workers, is under threat of demolition. The Amalgamated Society of Engineers, as the union was called when it was formed in 1851, bought land at the corner of Lyndhurst Road (now Way) and Peckham Road for £3,500 in 1899. The union's branches provided £30,000 to pay for the land and a new building. The Executive Council held its first meeting in Peckham on 1 October 1900. Plans dated 1914 show that there were originally three buildings along Peckham Road between Lyndhurst Road and Grummant Road. In 1916 they were joined together. The Amalgamated Society of Engineers' symbol, the slogan 'Be United And Industrious', 1851 and 1916 are carved above the doorway on the west side of the building. Apart from a six year confinement at Pitsford Hall, Northampton, during the Second World War when bombers blew the roof off the Peckham headquarters, the premises remained for nearly ninety years the general office of what became the Amalgamated Engineering and Electrical Union. A new administrative block was built in 1961 and the Executive Council block ten years later. Sir John Boyd, who was General Secretary of the AUEW, wrote: 'I always insisted that we make our large front garden as beautiful as possible for those who passed by to gaze upon – an oasis in a concrete jungle'. In 1912 a small chapel was at the Grummant Road side of what became the union's garden. The union left Peckham in 1996 and is now part of Amicus. The former front door of the Peckham building is now in the General Secretary's office in King Street, Covent Garden.

Right: *The Sons of Temperance offices in Blackfriars Road are seen here before the Second World War.*

Opposite: *The impressive headquarters of the Amalgamated Union of Engineering Workers is seen here in 1979.*

The Sons of Temperance is a Friendly Society that began in the nineteenth century and continues to promote the benefits of alcohol-free lifestyles. The building in Blackfriars Road is now the national headquarters of the organisation but it was built for the London Grand Division. Its boardroom includes an impressive photographic display of all its former chairmen known as Grand Worthy Patriarchs. In 1904 two large houses were purchased in Blackfriars Road. These were replaced by the present building that was opened by the Lord Mayor of London, Alderman Sir T. Vezey Strong, on 17 December 1910. The *South London Press* illustrated its report with a drawing of the building. At the opening ceremony, attended by a large number of dignitaries, the Grand Worthy Patriarch Brother C.H. Kemp said they were abundantly honoured that afternoon by the welcome presence of 'the first citizen of the first city in the world… What could be more appropriate than that the first teetotal Lord Mayor should open the first new offices of the first temperance friendly society?' The Lord Mayor was presented with a golden key and, in declaring the building open, he said that he appreciated the soundness and success of the organization. He stated that people who practised teetotalism enjoyed better health than those who drank alcohol. The Mayor of the Metropolitan Borough of Southwark, Cllr A. Wilson, said that the new headquarters was a credit to the organisation and an ornament to the borough. Information about the present activities and services provided by the Sons of Temperance can be obtained from 176 Blackfriars Road, SE1 8ET.

The first poppy factory was situated in Bermondsey.

The first poppy factory was situated in Bermondsey. In 1922 Major George Howson, an engineer who served on the Western Front in the First World War and who was awarded the Military Cross, founded The Disabled Society. With a grant of £2,000 from the Unity Relief Fund he set up a small factory in St James's Road, off the Old Kent Road, with five ex-servicemen who made the first British poppies. Within a few months, the number of employees had risen to fifty. The Disabled Society became a Limited Company and moved to larger premises at Richmond in Surrey, close to the site of the present poppy factory. From the small beginning in Bermondsey has grown today's factory whose mission remains – 'To organise, establish and manage schemes for the purpose of assisting men and women who have been members of the forces of the Crown, and primarily those of them who have been disabled while serving in such Forces or as a result of such service, together with the widows and disabled dependants of such ex-servicemen, by providing them with work provided they are physically capable thereof and with payment therefore'. The poppy factory now employs about seventy-five people, of whom almost 70 per cent are disabled, making mainly poppies and wreaths needed for the Poppy Appeal each November. In addition, there are over 100 home-workers who are provided with component parts to assemble the basic poppy emblem. The home-workers are mostly housebound by either chronic sickness or disability. There are other people either in residential homes or groups for disabled people who also assemble poppies. A free leaflet giving more information can be obtained from the Royal British Legion Poppy Factory Ltd, No. 20 Petersham Road, Richmond, Surrey TW10 6UR.

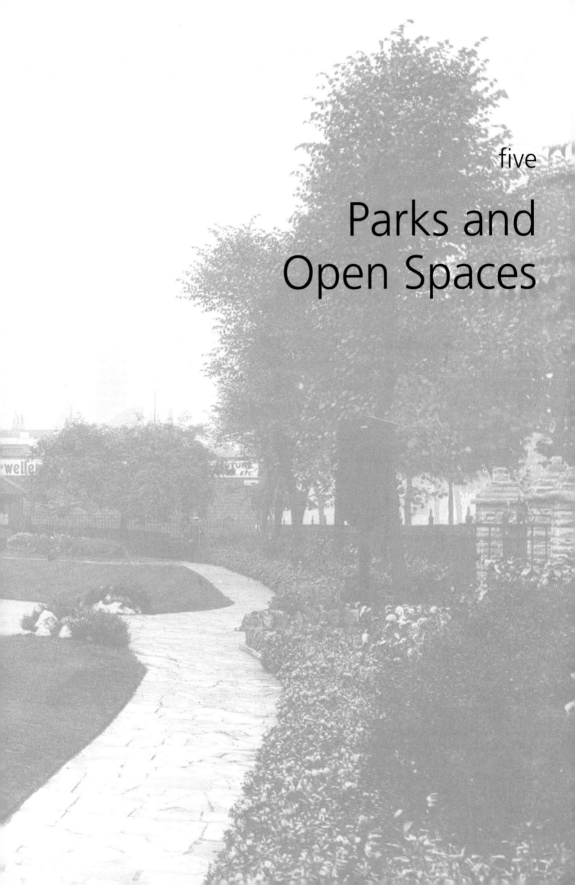

five

Parks and
Open Spaces

Goose Green was the village green of East Dulwich. No evidence exists to prove the origin of the name Goose Green. Long ago the land was connected to Peckham Rye Common. It was part of the manor of Camberwell Friern and was purchased as an open space in 1868 by Camberwell Vestry. This ran local affairs in the nineteenth century and was superseded by Camberwell Borough Council in 1900. A Mrs Dench kept donkeys and geese on the green. A pound for stray animals is shown on Dewhirst's 1842 map. A drinking fountain was erected on the green in commemoration of the Golden Jubilee of Queen Victoria (1887). In *Memories of the good and bad old days of childhood contributed by some East Dulwich people*, Elsie Stukings wrote: 'When the war years came in 1914 we children used to look through high railings around Goose Green and watch the soldiers drilling, and there were horses and tents as well'. The mural *William Blake's Vision of Angels*, on the wall adjacent to the children's playground (built in 1937-38), was painted in 1993 by Stan Peskett assisted by local schoolchildren, adults with learning difficulties and other community volunteers. The mural commemorates the vision of angels that William Blake (1757-1827), the visionary poet and painter, had as a child on Peckham Rye. There he had his first vision, of 'a tree filled with angels, bright angelic wings bespangling every bough like stars'. In the mural, Blake looks out on to an Arcadian sunset at a tree full of angels singing. Below him flows the River of Life, which represents themes of social justice and cultural and racial harmony. On the banks of the River are the Trees of Life, the leaves of which bring healing to all nations.

Right: *Around 1900 the bandstand was a popular feature in Southwark Park.*

Opposite: *Early in the twentieth century the former village green of East Dulwich had small trees on it.*

Southwark Park had a new bandstand in 2002, which was a replica of an old one from the same park. The park opened in 1869 but the original plans did not include a bandstand or provision for the playing of music. At the formal opening of the park, the bands of the 10th (Bermondsey) and 23rd (Rotherhithe) Surrey Rifle Volunteers played as part of the ceremony. A local firm called Hammer's had a band that began to play in the park. The firm provided a bandstand in the early 1880s. The Metropolitan Board of Works, who owned Southwark Park, gave permission in 1882 for music to be performed on Sundays. Later that year it reported that 'it is desirable, in order to prevent the bandstand in Southwark Park being used for objectionable purposes, that it should be surrounded with unclimbable iron hurdles'. The following year the MBW gave permission for a permanent bandstand. This was moved to Plumstead Common after a larger one was transferred in 1889 from the Royal Horticultural Society's gardens in South Kensington. Another from there was moved to Peckham Rye Common. A replica of these two still stands on Clapham Common. The bandstand was well used over many years. In 1919 the Royal Arsenal Co-operative Society held its children's sports day in the park. There was an evening concert in the bandstand from where Herbert Morrison, chairman of the London Labour Party, delivered an address on the importance of the Co-operative Movement. An incendiary bomb fell on the bandstand in 1940, but fortunately it was extinguished before much damage could be done. A historian who has traced the history of bandstands in Southwark Park has failed to discover what happened to the one that existed during the Second World War. It is hoped that a reader can provide this missing information. *Southwark Park: a brief history* by Pat Kingwell and Land Use Consultants is available from Southwark Local Studies Library.

Unusual houses and a public garden are hidden close to the busy Borough High Street. Red Cross Gardens in Redcross Way was laid out in 1887 by Julia, Countess of Ducie. The land was bought for £1,000 by Octavia Hill, a noted housing reformer, who wanted a nice park to be created in one of the worst slum areas in London. A paper factory had occupied the site before it was burnt down. A plaque was erected by Octavia Hill in 1896, which can be seen on a building next to the houses overlooking the little park. A book published in 1903 called *Living London* (edited by George R. Sims) referred to 'increasing and beautifying for the recreation of its citizens the hitherto neglected little plots of ground' and stated: 'In Red Cross Gardens, Southwark, is a good specimen of this valuable work, for there, in spite of the high buildings that surround this oasis on every side, can the inhabitants of that crowded part of the city rest in the open air in comparative quiet'. Red Cross Gardens is included in *The Story of Bankside* by Leonard Reilly and Geoff Marshall. The book refers to the idealism and determination shown by Octavia Hill who was responsible for the housing built on land owned by the Church of England in north Southwark. Before her time, the housing that had been built on this land by private landlords was usually of a very poor quality. When the leases expired, Octavia Hill arranged for the properties to be demolished. They were replaced by cottage-type buildings in a rustic style. Further examples of her work are White Cross Cottages in Ayers Street (1890) and Winchester Cottages in Copperfield Street (1894).

Right: *The fountain in Leyton Square no longer exists.*

Opposite: *The houses in Red Cross Gardens were photographed, c. 1935.*

England footballer Rio Ferdinand was born in King's College Hospital on 7 November 1978 and then lived at No. 18 Gisburn House on the Friary Estate in Peckham for eighteen years. He spent part of his leisure time in the nearby Leyton Gardens Adventure Playground. Leyton Square Public Garden was opened on 26 June 1901 by the Earl of Meath. He, as Lord Brabazon, founded the Metropolitan Public Gardens Association in 1882. The opening ceremony was presided over by the Mayor of Camberwell, Cllr Matthew Wallace. One of the guests was Mr J. Passmore Edwards, an editor and philanthropist, who provided a drinking fountain. The cost of acquiring the square for public use was £3,000; this was contributed by the Camberwell Vestry (which ran local affairs in the nineteenth century) and the London County Council. In its report on the opening of Leyton Square Garden, the *South London Press* said it was situated in 'one of the most popular parts of North Peckham'. The laying out of the ground was done by the Metropolitan Public Gardens Association; this cost about £600. Half was paid by Camberwell Borough Council (which took over from Camberwell Vestry in 1900) and the remainder was obtained for the MPGA from the London Parochial Charities. When the late Norman Hutchison spoke at a Camberwell Society meeting in 1998, he talked about Leyton Square and stated that it is protected by the London Squares Preservation Act 1931. This Act was based on recommendations of a Royal Commission that public and private open spaces needed protection against being built on. When redevelopment of that part of Peckham took place, the London County Council in an Act of 1952 had the land fronting Peckham Park Road made subject to the protective provisions of the 1931 Act.

This 1983 view of Brenchley Gardens shows where trains ran until 1954.

Brenchley Gardens were opened on 6 October 1928 by the Mayor of Camberwell, Cllr H.C. Thompson. The gardens were named after Cllr William Brenchley and were created on land occupied by allotments. The gardens were extended after adjacent railway tracks were lifted in 1956 following the closure of the line from Nunhead to Crystal Palace High Level Station in September 1954. Remnants of the lineside trees still exist – hybrid black poplars, ashes, aspen and sycamores. The *South London Press* reported the 'New open space for South London' in its 5 October 1928 issue saying: 'Nestling at the foot of One Tree Hill, Honor Oak, a pretty garden, simple in design, is rapidly taking shape... This Garden is situated in Forest Hill-rd and the Road Without a Name, and lies parallel with the railway as far as Kelvington-rd'. The 'nameless' road became Brenchley Gardens SE23; and when the gardens were opened they were only half completed. William Brenchley was born in Stepney but spent almost fifty years in public service in Camberwell. He was a member of the Camberwell Vestry before the Camberwell Borough Council was established in 1900. He served on the new Council and was Mayor in 1911-12. Brenchley Gardens, with a picture taken in springtime, are included in *East Dulwich: An Illustrated Alphabetical Guide*. The gardens also appear in 'from the Nun's Head to the Screaming Alice: a green walk along the old Crystal Palace (High Level) railway' (Friends of the Great North Wood) and *The Parks and Woodlands of London* by Andrew Crowe (Fourth Estate). William Brenchley is one of over 125 people in *Who Was Who in Peckham* (Chener Books).

David Copperfield Garden is pictured in the year it opened, 1932.

David Copperfield Garden in the New Kent Road was named after one of the best-known characters created by the nineteenth century novelist Charles Dickens. In *David Copperfield* (Chapter 13) the young David walked from London to Dover to find his aunt. He wrote: 'I came to a stop in the Kent Road, at a terrace with a piece of water before it, and a great foolish image in the middle, blowing a dry shell'. This quote from the novel is inscribed on a memorial in the garden at New Kent Road. On 9 February 1932, the *South London Press* reported the unveiling by the novelist Horace Annesley Vachell. Standing on the plinth of stone was a figure of a boy vainly trying to obtain a drink of water from a shell. Beneath is the inscription: 'To connect this spot with the flight of David Copperfield to his aunt's at Dover. This plaque has been placed by the Dickens Fellowship'. Mr Vachell, President of the Fellowship, said that personal experience was the true touchstone that made a novel endure. He declared that Charles Dickens dipped his quill into his heart's blood when he wrote *David Copperfield*. *Charles Dickens and Southwark*, published by Southwark Local Studies Library, states that the terrace referred to in *David Copperfield* was Webb's County Terrace. The piece of water and the image disappeared in the 1880s. *Charles Dickens and Southwark* tells the story of the author's links with what today is the London Borough of Southwark, using the author's own words where possible; he was born on 7 February 1812 and died on 9 June 1870. In 1824, Charles Dickens's father, John, was imprisoned for debt in Marshalsea Prison. One prison wall still exists, next to Southwark Local Studies Library that was built where John Dickens was a prisoner.

In 1977 a photograph was taken of All Hallows' Garden in Copperfield Street where the church used to be.

In Copperfield Street, named after the eponymous Dickensian hero, is the lovely All Hallows' Garden, which includes a fig tree. Opposite is a charming row of cottages built by the church owners in 1885. This end of Copperfield Street, formerly known as Norfolk Street, was described in an 1861 report as 'the most notorious thoroughfare in the district'. The beautiful garden, which is a summer haven for office workers, was created on the site of the former All Hallows' church whose history was brief but worthy of record. An old lady called Mrs Hunt left £10,000 for the church. Construction began in 1879 from the designs of George Gilbert Scott (1839-97), father of Sir Giles Gilbert Scott (1880-1960) the designer of Bankside Power Station, which later became Tate Modern. The church's architect was the eldest son of Sir George Gilbert Scott (1811-78) and was sometimes described as the most brilliant of the Scott dynasty of architects. Sadly he was afflicted with mental illness and at one time was committed to Bethlem Hospital (which is now used by the Imperial War Museum). As one sits in the tranquil garden, it is hard to imagine that on the small site stood the lofty Gothic style church accommodating 1,200 people. It was once one of the largest churches in London with an interior length of 150ft with side aisles of 90ft and basement rooms. All Hollows' was gutted by incendiary fires in 1941. A chancel aisle on the north side then formed a side chapel that was restored for services until 1971 when the congregation united with that of Southwark Cathedral.

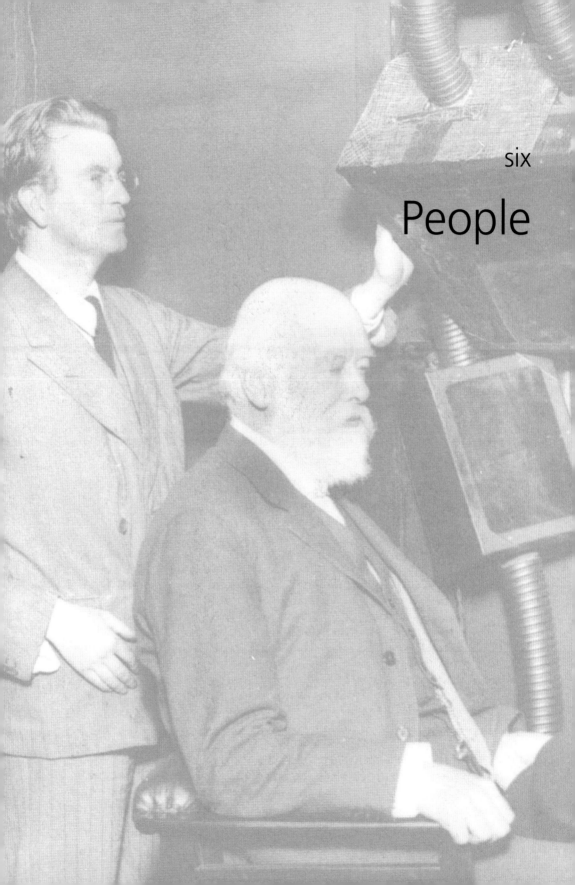

six

People

The Burial Ground in Dulwich Village, at the junction of Court Lane and Calton Avenue, was consecrated in 1616. Despite being enlarged twice, it was full by 1858. In *Ye Parish of Camerwell* published in 1875, W.H. Blanch wrote: 'The College burial-ground is not now used, except by special permission'. In the appendix to his book, Blanch included an account of the consecration of the Burial Ground by Archbishop Abbot on 1 September 1616 in the presence of Edward Alleyn, founder of what today is Dulwich College. Among the people buried there are John Eggleton, described by Blanch as a 'player' whose wife was the original Lucy in the *Beggar's Opera*. Another actor who lies there is Anthony Boheme, 'the famous tragedian'. 'Old Bridgett, the Queen of the Gypsies' was buried in 1768. Samuel Matthews, called the 'Dulwich Hermit' and who was murdered in his cave adjoining Sydenham Common, was buried in 1803. Mathematician Thomas Jones, who was a fellow and tutor of Trinity College, Cambridge, was laid to rest in 1807 in a vault 'for one person, 8ft x 2ft'. The curious fact is recorded that after the funeral the 'undertaker left 8 shillings for the boys for singing before the coffin'. Another person buried there is the solicitor Richard Shaw who had Casino House erected in 1796. (Sunray Gardens were part of the beautiful grounds.) He was solicitor to Warren Hastings, Governor-General of India, during his 145-day trial in 1795, which resulted in an acquittal. Thirty-five Dulwich plague victims are also buried here. In the early part of the nineteenth century there were several incidents of attempted body snatching from freshly dug graves. A free leaflet, *In & Around Dulwich*, obtainable from Southwark Local Studies Library, details Richard Shaw's tomb.

Right: *Richard Cuming founded the museum in Walworth Road.*

Opposite: *This picture of the Burial Ground in Dulwich Village was taken in 1952.*

A water pump from Marshalsea Prison, where Charles Dickens' father was an inmate (because of debt) is in the Cuming Museum This is run by Southwark Council and is in the same building as Newington Library in Walworth Road. The founder of the museum was Richard Cuming (1777-1870). He and his son Henry Syer Cuming (1817-1902) gathered an amazing number of objects from around the world. The Cuming collection began in 1782 when a Mrs Coleman of Manor Place, Walworth, gave five-year-old Richard a copper coin from India and three pieces of fossil. He made his own cardboard cabinet for these and other curiosities in 1791. By the early 1800s he was beginning to buy objects at public sales. His house in Walworth soon housed his own museum. After his son Henry's death, the contents of the museum became the property of the Metropolitan Borough of Southwark. All the items were removed from the Cuming home in Kennington Park Road to Newington Library in 1903 at a cost of only £6. A room was added to the existing library to house the Cuming collection. The museum was opened on 10 October 1906 with the official ceremony being performed by Lord Rothschild. Many items have been added to the Cuming Museum since it was opened. Special exhibitions are held and this important free resource is widely used by children and adults. Nearly a century after the museum opened, a colourful book was published telling the unusual story of the Cuming family and highlighting some of the important and interesting items housed in the Cuming Museum. *An Introduction to the Cuming Family and the Cuming Museum* by Stephen Humphrey can be obtained from Southwark Local Studies Library.

Dr John Scott Lidgett was the founder of the Bermondsey Settlement.

Scott Lidgett Crescent, close to where the Bermondsey Settlement was opened in 1892, commemorates a remarkable man who founded this important institution. Fifty years after the death of Dr John Scott Lidgett (1854-1953), a full length biography was published. Though most of Dr Lidgett's own papers were lost years ago, Dr Alan Turberfield succeeded in writing a comprehensive history of a notable clergyman who has been described as the greatest Methodist since John Wesley, founder of this branch of the Christian church. Dr Lidgett founded the Bermondsey Settlement to provide opportunities for educationally privileged people to serve the needs of poor people in a wide range of religious, educational and social activities. An early resident was Dr Alfred Salter who met his future wife, Ada, at the Settlement. Dr Salter was a highly respected GP and MP in Bermondsey. Ada Salter was the first woman councillor in London. Scott Lidgett was warden of the Bermondsey Settlement for fifty-seven years. After many years of vital service to people and the community, the settlement closed in 1967. Dr Lidgett was leader of the Progressive Party on the London County Council, Vice-Chancellor of London University, Chairman of the Executive Committee of the Central Council for Nursing and the first President of the Methodist Conference after the 1932 unification of the three strands of Methodism. This remarkable man packed much into his ninety–eight years. Dr Turberfield's thorough biography filled a gap in books on people who have played a major part in what today is the London Borough of Southwark. *John Scott Lidgett: Archbishop of British Methodism?* by Alan Turberfield is published by Epworth Press. A copy can be seen in Southwark Local Studies Library where there are photographs of Dr Lidgett and the Bermondsey Settlement.

In 1980 Sir George Livesey's statue was in the grounds of the gasworks in the Old Kent Road.

Peckham's only statue can be seen in the courtyard of the Livesey Museum in the Old Kent Road. It commemorates Sir George Livesey (1834-1908) and was moved there from the gasworks across the road. The museum was originally the first public library in the Metropolitan Borough of Camberwell. It was a gift to the people of Peckham from George Livesey in 1890. George Livesey was buried in Nunhead Cemetery where his grave is a prominent feature. He was a son of Thomas Livesey who was employed by the Gas Light and Coke Co. from 1821. In 1839 Thomas became chief clerk of the South Metropolitan Gas Co. and lived close to their works in the Old Kent Road. George Livesey started working for the SMGC in 1848 and became his father's assistant. He was made engineer to the company in 1862 and, on his father's death in 1871, George became secretary of the company and later the chairman of the board of directors. The building and operation of the gasworks in the Old Kent Road date from 1829. Gas making appears to have begun in 1833. Two gas holders, built in the 1870s, are still in use even though the fine office block and the entrance gate are let to other interests. Christ Church, next to the Livesey Museum, was built after the original church on the other side of the Old Kent Road was demolished because the gasworks needed to expand. The church has iron gas pipes as pillars. George Livesey and the Peckham gasworks are included in a book by Dr Mary Mills called *Places and People in the Early East London Gas* Industry; it includes over 200 illustrations.

The scouts' funeral procession went through Peckham on 10 August 1912. This photograph was taken from the roof of Corsbie's Fancy Repository, Nos 217-219 Rye Lane.

When eight scouts were drowned in the Thames in 1912 an impressive funeral was held at Nunhead Cemetery. A Mourning Scout memorial, erected in memory of the boys lost, was vandalised in 1969 and has since been replaced by a new monument. The first scout camp was held in 1907 on Brownsea Island in Poole Harbour, Dorset. It was organised by Lt-Gen Robert Baden-Powell, the hero of the South African War. Scouting soon symbolised a new vision and motivation for youth. A scout troop was formed at St John's church, Larcom Street in Walworth. The scoutmaster of the 2nd Walworth Troop, Sidney John Marsh, was an ex-Dulwich College boy and a licensed lay reader attached to the Dulwich College Mission. He took his troop for a camp at Leysdown in 1911, which was a great success, and another camp was organised the following year. Because the troop had attained a high standard of seamanship, they were chosen to give a display at the Sea Scout Rally at Earls Court a month before the 1912 camp. The scouts set off in August along the Thames from Waterloo Bridge heading towards Leysdown. The sails were hoisted after passing Tower Bridge. Eventually, after battling with wind and rain, the scouts were only two miles from their destination. Then tragedy struck. A squall caught the boat, which keeled over and the scouts were thrown into the water. The Leysdown Coastguards rowed out through the heavy sea in their little gig. Sadly, the rescuers arrived too late to save eight of the scouts but with great difficulty they managed to save some scouts and Sidney Marsh. The whole moving story has been told by Rex Batten in *The Walworth Scouts* which is available from the Friends of Nunhead Cemetery.

Dr Harold Moody was a highly regarded GP.

Peckham's newest park is named after Dr Harold Moody and the only English Heritage blue plaque in SE15 commemorates him. This can be seen at No. 164 Queens Road where he lived and worked. In 1904 Harold Moody came to London from Jamaica, where he was born in 1882. He studied medicine at King's College and qualified as a doctor. He was invited to preach at Clifton Congregational church (where Clifton Court in Asylum Road is today). The people of Peckham took to Dr Moody and he liked them. Consequently, in 1913, he set up in practice as a doctor at No. 111 King's Road (now Grove). Dr Moody was concerned about the discrimination experienced by black people in Britain before the Second World War. In 1931 he formed the League of Coloured Peoples which became very influential and his home became the base for the league's activities. In 1933 Dr Moody was invited by the Lord Mayor of Hull to co-operate in the civic commemoration of the centenary of the death of anti-slave campaigner William Wilberforce. Harold Moody's speech at the Commemoration Dinner made a great impression. Dr Moody's funeral service in 1947 was held in Camberwell Green Congregational church, Wren Road, where he had long been a member. The service was attended by a large number of people from many walks of life including leaders in the religious, political and social life of Britain and the Commonwealth. Dr Moody's former patients speak with much gratitude of the caring GP they knew when they were young. Harold Moody is included in *Southwark: Who Was Who* by Shirley Harrison and Sally Evemy which can be obtained from Southwark Local Studies Library where *Negro Victory: The life story of Dr Harold Moody* by David A. Vaughan can also be found. A new biography of Dr Moody is being written by Professor David Killingray and is due to be published in 2005.

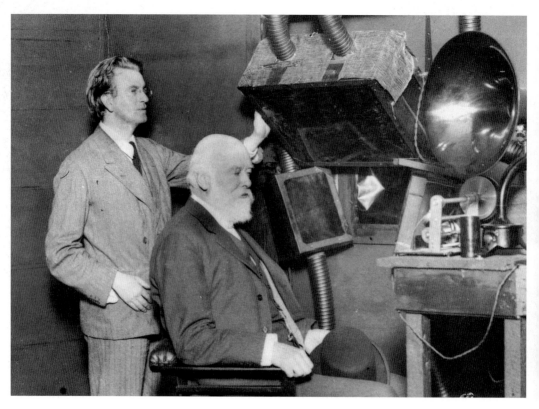

John Logie Baird stands next to Sir Oliver Lodge, c. 1930.

Television pioneer John Logie Baird (1888-1946) lived in Dulwich. Though born in Scotland, he was driven south by poor health. From an attic in Hastings he made the world's first practical television transmission in 1924. He followed this in 1926 with the first public demonstration at his new workshop in Soho. In 1928 he transmitted television over the Atlantic. The BBC inaugurated an experimental service in 1929 using one of the Crystal Palace towers to carry the aerials. John Logie Baird was attracted to the high towers of the Crystal Palace, so in 1934 he moved to No. 3 Crescent Wood Road, SE26. He stayed there until 1946. He set up a studio in the South Tower where he experimented with ultra short-wave and colour transmissions. A government committee was set up in 1936 to adjudicate between John Baird's part-mechanical 240-line system and Marconi-EMI's rival all electronic 405-line system. Unfortunately for Mr Baird, the committee recommended the rival system as it probably would have done even if he had not been unfortunate enough to lose vital equipment in the fire that destroyed the Crystal Palace later that year. His inferior system was at the limit of its potential achievement. Mystery surrounds John Baird's work in his last few years. He may have been engaged on secret work involving radar and the high speed transmission of printed and filmed material. John Logie Baird is one of a hundred notable people included in *Who Was Who in Dulwich*. The television pioneer is also mentioned in Brian Green's book *Dulwich: A History*.

The drive in the grounds of Peckham House is seen here, c. 1935.

Charlie Chaplin's mother, Hannah Chaplin, was transferred from Cane Hill Asylum to Peckham House in Peckham Road on 9 September 1912. This was a private lunatic asylum and stood where The Academy at Peckham is today. In the London Metropolitan Archives are receipts of Peckham House showing that, in May 1915, the proprietors applied for her to be given financial assistance under the Poor Law because Charlie and his brother Sydney had defaulted in paying the fees of 30s a week for their mother. Hannah Chaplin was a vaudeville artist until her voice failed. Impoverished and malnourished, she alternated between shabby rooms in Kennington, Lambeth workhouse and the public asylum at Cane Hill in Surrey. According to Kenneth Lynn in *Charlie Chaplin and His Times*, she was 'a figure of tragic intensity … a woman of sorrows'. The transfer to Peckham House followed a visit of Sydney and Charlie to Cane Hill. Peckham House was previously a mansion owned by Charles Lewis Spitta. The wealthy Spitta family lived there in great style, giving fetes for their neighbours and dispensing charity to poor people in the district. It became a lunatic asylum in 1826 and closed in 1951 so Peckham School could be built on the site; Dame Norma Major, wife of former Prime Minister John Major, was a pupil there. *Who Was Who in Peckham* includes Baroness Summerskill who married Dr E. Jeffrey Samuel. At the time of their marriage in 1925 he was a medical officer at Peckham House. Edith Summerskill wrote in her memoirs *A Woman's World*: 'I was a frequent visitor to the hospital – indeed it provided a background for our courting and we never failed to join in the Christmas festivities for many years after my husband had left'.

Eveline Lowe was chairman of the London County Council in 1939.

Eveline Lowe School in SE1 commemorates the first woman chairman of the London County Council. She was a prominent social worker and administrator in South London. She was born in Rotherhithe in 1869 and was the daughter of a Congregational Minister, the Revd J. Farren. She trained as a teacher and early in life she joined the staff of Homerton College in Cambridge. She later became Vice-Principal. Eveline married Dr George Lowe. He was a distinguished physician who was in partnership with Bermondsey's famous GP and MP, Dr Alfred Salter. Eveline and George formed the Bermondsey Independent Labour Party with the co-operation of other activists from local chapels. Eveline became actively involved in local government and served as a Bermondsey Borough Councillor and a member of the education committee. From 1922 until 1946 she sat for Bermondsey as a Labour member of the London County Council. She was appointed deputy chairman in 1929 and chairman in 1939. Eveline Lowe was chairman of the governors at James Allen's Girls' School and Honor Oak Girls' School. A portrait of her by A.K. Lawrence used to hang in the Ayes Lobby at County Hall. After the Second World War she lived at 30 Dulwich Common until she died in 1956. Her personal papers are in the Women's Library at London Guildhall University. Eveline Lowe is one of a hundred notable people included in *Who Was Who in Dulwich*. She and her husband are also featured in *Bermondsey Story: The Life of Alfred Salter* by Fenner Brockway.

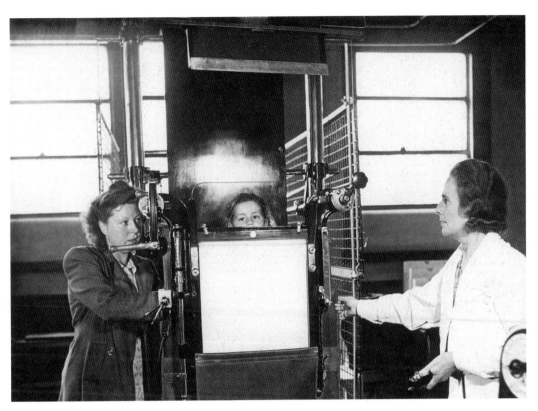

Nurse Janet Jack X-rays a girl's chest.

Jessie (known as Janet) Jack (1906-2000) worked at the Public Health Centre in Grange Road, Bermondsey, as a radiographer. She was in charge of the X-ray department that dealt with many people suffering from tuberculosis. She went to great lengths to obtain the newest equipment available. She encouraged whole families to be X-rayed and used to deliver reports to doctors' surgeries each evening on her way home. When the X-ray unit in the Public Health Centre closed, Janet was put in charge of the X-ray department at St Olave's Hospital, Rotherhithe. She often had to deal with dockers' injuries and drunken merchant seamen who had head injuries. Doctors wondered how she controlled such large strong men until she admitted that she had a secret weapon – the local Roman Catholic priest who, Janet said, put the fear of God into them! Janet was born in Morayshire, Scotland, and moved to Malvern in England when she was sixteen. She persuaded a local hospital matron to allow her to train as a nurse when she was old enough. Though she was small and weak, she was allowed to work on the wards to prove she could lift patients and make beds. Janet qualified as a State Registered Nurse and as a midwife. She was a volunteer in the Red Cross and was at Olympia in 1976 when an IRA bomb exploded. Her photograph appeared in a national newspaper that described her as a heroine. Janet was an active member of Bermondsey Central Hall where her life of dedicated service was acknowledged at her funeral. Southwark Local Studies Library has a number of Bermondsey Health Centre photographs taken by Pictorial Press, which started in 1938, and is now based at Unit 1, Market Yard Mews, 194 Bermondsey Street, SE1 3TQ.

Barry Albin-Dyer sits in front of a painting of one of Britain's oldest funeral firms. In the centre of the back row is Barry Albin-Dyer with his sons (Simon, left, and Jonathan, right). In the front row are Barry's father (George Dyer, left) and Fred Albin (holding the pen).

Don't Drop the Coffin, Final Departures and Bury My Heart in Bermondsey by Barry Albin-Dyer reveal the funny and frightening experiences he has had as an undertaker. He runs F.A. Albin & Sons, based in Bermondsey, which was officially established in 1842 but was in existence for some forty to sixty years before that. The firm's Funeral Home in Culling Road was built in 1974 on the site of the Old Runge Hall. F.A. Albin's have been involved in funerals in Bermondsey since the late eighteenth century when it is believed they were wardens of a cemetery. They are one of the oldest independent firms of funeral directors. When Barry Albin-Dyer was very young, Albin's had four funeral shops, as they were known then. The Bermondsey shop was in Snowsfield and later at No. 62 Jamaica Road. His father was the senior manager. Fred, Ernie and Arthur Albin were the joint owners. The garage, where hearses and limousines were kept, was in railway arches on Southwark Park Road. On the wall at the rear of the Jamaica Road shop, facing the London Bridge to Kent railway line, was written in black letters on a white background: 'F.A. Albin & Sons. Funeral Directors. Burials and Cremations. Embalming Available'. Barry was frightened of death in those days and his friends would not go to his home to play with him because he lived in a funeral home. At the age of nine Barry was given a summer holiday job at Albin's. He cleaned the cars and learnt how to make coffins in the workshop for stillborn babies. He also put mouldings on adult coffins and French polished them with linseed oil.

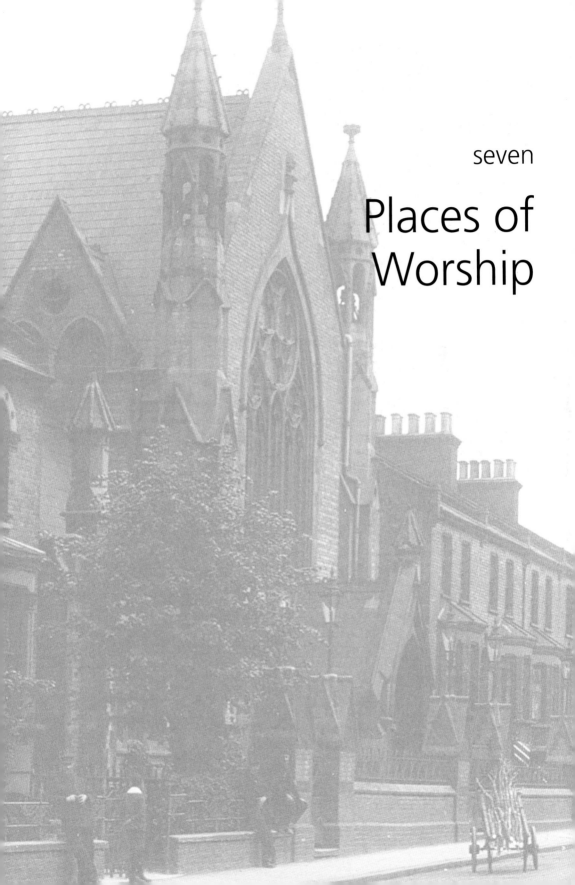

seven

Places of
Worship

Christ's Chapel of Alleyn's College of God's Gift at Dulwich, in College Road, is the full title of the Foundation Chapel, which serves not only the three Foundation Schools (Dulwich College, Alleyn's School and James Allen's Girls' School), but also the residents of the Almshouses (now Edward Alleyn House) and other inhabitants of Dulwich who wish to worship there. On 17 May 1613 Edward Alleyn signed a contract with John Benson, bricklayer of Westminster, for the building of his college, the central part of which was to be the chapel. This took three years to build. The Revd Cornelius Lymer, Chaplain of Christ Church at Oxford, was appointed as Chaplain on 31 August 1616. The following day, on Edward Alleyn's fiftieth birthday, the chapel was consecrated by George Abbot, Archbishop of Canterbury. On the same day he consecrated the Burial Ground at the other end of Dulwich village. The many distinguished visitors on that day included Francis Bacon, Lord Chancellor. Three years later, on 21 June 1619, Francis Bacon issued the Letters Patent on behalf of King James I to Edward Alleyn officially to enable him to create The College of God's Gift. The Archbishop of Canterbury became The Visitor to the Foundation, a post held by all his successors. Gilbert Sheldon became Archbishop of Canterbury in 1663 and was shocked to find that a detachment of soldiers from Fairfax's army had been quartered at the chapel and had 'committed great havoc'. The Revd James Hume was the author of the Latin inscription over the porch at the chapel entrance which, in translation, concludes: 'Blessed is he who takes pity on the poor, go thou and do likewise'. A booklet giving the history of Christ's Chapel was written by Arthur R. Chandler.

Right: *The Pilgrim Fathers' Memorial church is seen here in about 1920.*

Opposite: *The interior of Christ's Chapel was photographed in 1920.*

Pilgrim Fathers sailed in the *Mayflower* from Rotherhithe in 1620 to New England (in what today is the USA) in search of religious freedom. A plaque in a small public garden near the Bricklayers Arms flyover in the New Kent Road commemorates this event. The ship's captain, Christopher Jones, returned to England the year after the voyage. He died in 1622 and was buried in the churchyard of his parish, St Mary's, where there is a modern memorial inside the Rotherhithe church. The story of the Pilgrim Fathers goes back to 1571 when a group of people were imprisoned in London's Bridewell prison because they refused to obey the Uniformity Act of Elizabeth I. They objected to having to use the Book of Common Prayer in services. They held their own services of worship even in the prison. In 1586 a similar group of people was held captive in the infamous Clink prison which was part of the Bishop of Winchester's Palace. (A wall and fourteenth century window can still be seen in Clink Street.) They too held their own kind of worship and formed a prison church. Some of the people involved started the Southwark Independent church. The Pilgrim Fathers' Memorial church claims to be descended from it. The present church, opened in 1956, is in Great Dover Street. This replaced one opened in 1864 in Buckenham Square off the New Kent Road. This was destroyed in 1941 by enemy action. More information is included in *The Mayflower and Pilgrim Story* by Mary Boast, *The Story of Rotherhithe* by Stephen Humphrey and *Southwark: An Illustrated History* by Leonard Reilly all published by Southwark Local Studies Library.

Left: *In 1799 St John's church, Horselydown, was a prominent feature in the neighbourhood.*

Opposite: *A sketch was made in about 1850 of the Friends' Meeting House.*

S treets *Paved With Gold* is the title of a book telling the story of the London City Mission. The headquarters are near Tower Bridge on the site of St John Horselydown church which was consecrated in 1733. It was one of the last works of the Commission for Building Fifty New Churches. This body, which in fact managed only fifteen churches, was set up in Queen Anne's reign by the Tories who were anxious to rescue the suburbs from the clutches of Nonconformity. By 1734 the Whigs had long been in power, money was short, and for St John's church the commissioners ordered a cut-price job from their two surveyors – Nicholas Hawksmoor and John James. The parsonage, which still exists, was designed by Hawksmoor in 1733. A great disturbance happened in the church in 1737. Some women in the congregation were wearing prohibited India silk and callico gowns and informers went looking for them. However, the women were tipped off and went into the vestry to change their clothes. To protect England's textiles industry, an Act of Parliament had been passed in 1700 prohibiting the use and wearing of Asian textiles. The 150th anniversary of the church was celebrated in 1883. The *South London Press* reported on 16 August that a public luncheon was held in the large hall of St Olave's Grammar School presided over by the Rt Hon. A.J.B. Beresford Hope, MP. The church was burned in an air raid in 1940. The famous 225ft spire was taken down in 1948. The tower had a weather vane shaped like a comet. From the ground it looked like a large insect which gave the church its local name of 'Louse Church'.

The oldest part of the Royal Mail Delivery Office near Peckham Rye Station was a Quaker Meeting House. In a book on Camberwell and Neighbourhood published in 1841, Douglas Allport wrote: 'In Hanover street [now Highshore Road], Peckham, the Society of Friends have a substantial and well-built meeting house, with commodious vestry-rooms adjoining. It has a screen of trees before it, is enclosed by a wall and gates, and exhibits a respectable and characteristic appearance... It was erected in 1825; the respected members of this body having been accustomed to meet for worship at a house in Harder's Road, for about four years previous to that time'. Among the people who worshipped in the Meeting House were William Bryant and Francis May who formed the famous match-making firm. Dame Elizabeth Cadbury was married in the Meeting House. She was Elizabeth Mary Taylor when she was born at Peckham Rye in 1858 and she married chocolate manufacturer George Cadbury in 1888. Astronomer Sir Arthur Stanley Eddington, who was chief assistant at the Greenwich Observatory, worshipped there as did Dr Alfred Salter and his wife Ada. Another worshipper was Sir John (H.) Harris, Secretary to the Anti-Slavery and Aborigines Protection Society. The Meeting House closed in 1961. More information about the Quaker Meeting House and its worshippers is included in *Southwark's Burying Places* by Ron Woollacott, *Bermondsey Story* by Fenner Brockway, *Peckham and Nunhead Churches* and *Who Was Who in Peckham*.

A German Lutheran church used to be situated in Windsor Walk.

A German Lutheran church was opened in 1855 close to where Denmark Hill Station is today. It was built on land belonging to Sir Claude de Crespigny. The church was big enough to seat about 300 people. Services were conducted entirely in German. The clergyman had to be ordained by the German Protestant church, and was elected by the members for life. Everyone who subscribed for one year had a vote. The chancel windows were filled with stained glass. Inside were open benches made from deal that was lightly stained and varnished. Oak was used to make the pulpit. The gas fittings were very decorative. A drawing of the church was published in *The Illustrated London News* on 29 November 1856. The congregation first met for worship in Camberwell in Dr Crofts' school in 1854. The church, which was in Windsor Walk, was vacated by the German congregation in 1914. From the 1920s it was used by Open Brethren who called it Beresford church. The first reference to Germans in Camberwell was in a curious little pamphlet published in 1710 called *The State of the Palatines for fifty years past to this present time*. It is one of the oldest items in Southwark Local Studies Library and includes a picture of German Protestant refugees living in tents in Camberwell and Blackheath. About 9,000 had been forced to flee their homes in the former German state of The Palatinate. They were treated in a kind way in Camberwell. Information about the German church and the community it served is included in *The Story of Camberwell* by Mary Boast. The church is shown on the Ordnance Survey Map: Peckham 1894 (Alan Godfrey Maps).

Arsonists destroyed Peckham Methodist church in 1972.

Peckham Methodist church was destroyed by arson on 26 October 1972. The police never caught the two boys who set fire to the church, but some years later it was revealed that they had been pupils at Bredinghurst School, a boarding school for youngsters with special needs run by the Inner London Education Authority. The church had been sold to Quadrant Housing Association so flats could be built on the site at the corner of Queens Road and Harders (now Woods) Road. Walter Finch, after whom Finch Mews was named, suggested that the block of flats be called Cherry Tree Court because it was close to a cherry tree which stood outside the present church that opened in 1974. The tree, as a young sapling, had been carried on a No. 36 bus in about 1960 from an allotment in Crofton Park. It was planted in the front garden of No. 1 Harders Road. The church that was burnt had been opened in 1865. It replaced the 1834 Wesleyan Chapel which can still be seen in Staffordshire Street and is used by the Peckham Settlement. The Victorian church, with its spire which was a landmark in the area, was built on land which had partly been occupied by a boarding school for young ladies. The new chapel was opened by the President of the Wesleyan Conference, the Revd William L. Thornton; this was his last official engagement before his sudden death. An engraving of the new chapel, showing ladies wearing crinolines, was the first picture to appear in the news columns of the *Methodist Recorder*. The story of Peckham Methodist church is told in *Building Together* which includes a description of Peckham when it was a Surrey village.

The Catholic Apostolic church, seen here in around 1900, became a Greek Orthodox Cathedral.

St Mary's Greek Orthodox Cathedral in Camberwell New Road was originally a Catholic Apostolic church. It originated from a group led by the Revd N. Armstrong who acquired the use of Salem Chapel in Deverell Street (1834–35). From there the congregation moved to a building in Trinity Street (1835–73). The *South London Press* reported on Saturday 4 March 1876 that 'from various circumstances – such as the want of space, and the various changes which the neighbourhood underwent – it was deemed advisable to go farther afield'. The Camberwell church was opened on Thursday 2 March 1876 and the *South London Press* wrote a long description of the Early English style building and described the opening service which lasted for over three hours. There was seating for 650 people. The architects were J. & J. Belcher of Adelaide Place, London Bridge. This was a father and son partnership; both were named John. The son is included in the *Dictionary of National Biography*. He was born on 10 July 1841 at No. 3 Montague Terrace, Trinity Square, Southwark. John Belcher designed a house for himself called Redholm which was built in 1885. This still exists in Champion Hill, Camberwell, next to The Fox on the Hill. John Belcher was an Angel, the name given to a priest of the Catholic Apostolic Church. He died at Redholm on 8 November 1913. The Camberwell Catholic Apostolic Church was very badly damaged in 1943; part of the nave was destroyed. After the Second World War the Catholic Apostolic Church was virtually defunct but their church in Camberwell continued to have a congregation until 1961. The Greek Orthodox Church took over the building in 1963 on a peppercorn rent and finally bought it in 1977. Since then it has been a Cathedral so the London Borough of Southwark has three cathedrals.

The New Peckham Mosque in Camberwell's Cobourg Road, also known as Noorul Islam Turkish Mosque, is the former St Mark's church. The architect of the chancel, part of the nave and the south chancel aisle was Norman Shaw. He also designed New Scotland Yard, the former headquarters of the Metropolitan Police on the Victoria Embankment in Westminster. The Mosque was founded in 1984 by Shaikh Nazim Haqqani Naqshabandi who is of Turkish Cypriot origin. He is a well-known Sufi Master with many followers. St Mark's church was consecrated on 6 June 1880 but the building was not finished until 1932 because it took a long time to raise the money to build the part of the church facing the road. A photograph and report of the start of the completion was published in the *South London Press* on 16 October 1931. Under the completion stone a copy of the previous week's *South London Press* was put in a sealed steel box. The stone was laid by Mrs W.T. Partridge, wife of Dr Partridge, the churchwarden. The lady had been present when the foundation stone was laid fifty years earlier. Canon H.G. Veazey spent over forty years in St Mark's parish and was a member of Camberwell Borough Council. He worked hard to improve housing conditions. A memorial outside St Mark's church commemorated local men who died in the First World War and read: 'In proud and lasting memory of St Mark's Little Army, numbering 4,286. 524 laid down their lives – God bless them. May we and England be worthy of them.' The New Peckham Mosque is included in *The Mosques of London* by Fatima Gailani.

An Anglican church, seen here in 1985, became a Mosque.

The Copleston Centre, which does vital community work in Peckham, is based in the former St Saviour's church ('saint' is an adjective meaning holy, so the derivation of the church's name is 'Holy Saviour's'; there was no St Saviour) in Copleston Road, which was named after Edward Copleston (1776-1849), Bishop of Llandaff. While the church was being built in the nineteenth century, services were held at Waverley House, the house next door to the site, under the jurisdiction of the clergy of St John the Evangelist, East Dulwich, from which parish the new one was formed. These services were attended by a fair number of people considering the scarcity of houses in the immediate vicinity and also the condition of the roads, especially in bad weather. The consecration service was conducted by the Bishop of Rochester, Dr Anthony Thorold, on 22 February 1881. The church was paid for by the tea merchant Francis Peek. The first vicarage was what is now Bromar Court in Grove Hill Road. A leading figure in British academic musical life, Sir Jack Allan Westrup (1904-75), attended St Saviour's church and deputised as organist; he was brought up opposite the church at No. 46 Copleston Road in a house that has since been demolished. During the Second World War the church's east window was blown out and the organ was damaged. St Saviour's Anglican church amalgamated with Hanover United Reformed church, which began in the 1650s, and the Victorian building was converted into The Copleston Centre. Church House opposite, erected in 1902, was sold to help pay the cost; this is now used by the Latter-Rain Outpouring Revival Bethany. *The Copleston Story: A Celebration of The Copleston Centre 1978-2001* by Jackie Bowie can be obtained from The Copleston Centre, Copleston Road, SE15 4AN.

Right: *This is the only known photograph of Avondale Road Unitarian church.*

Opposite: *St Saviour's church, photographed in the early part of the twentieth century, became The Copleston Centre.*

No picture has been found of Avondale Road Unitarian church in Peckham, which was bombed during the Second World War but a photograph of its organ does exist. It is hoped that this will result in the discovery of a picture of the church's exterior. In *Peckham and Nunhead Remembered* Leonard Moncrieff wrote from Canada: 'The Unitarian church in Avondale Road (now Rise), which I attended for several years from the 1920s, seated about 150 people in centre pews and two sides. It had a very fine pipe organ with hand-pumped bellows. It had quite an ornate pulpit of carved wood. The church was lit by gas until electricity was installed. The Revd Magnus Ratter was the minister until he went to India. The church, hall and some houses were bombed in May 1941. My cousin and her baby were killed in the same air raid.' The book includes a picture of a children's Christmas party held in the Avondale Road church hall, in Bellenden Road, in December 1938. The church was opened on 13 December 1882 but the congregation dated from 1867 when the Revd George Carter started holding services in a small hall in Walworth. Five years later the congregation moved to a chapel in Alder Street, Peckham, which opened on Easter Sunday 1872. Three years later a move was made to Avondale Road where a small iron chapel was opened on 18 July 1875. A schoolroom was finished in 1881 and the new church was opened the following year. *Peckham and Nunhead Churches* includes the Unitarian church.

In about 1930, when this photograph was taken, the church was well used by Norwegian seamen.

A Norwegian church consecrated in 1927 stands near the entrance to Rotherhithe Tunnel. Prior to it being built, Norwegians established Ebenezer church in Redriff Road in 1871. At that time Norway was united to Sweden; the two countries separated in 1905. The present church was erected by Norwegian shipowners as a memorial to 2,101 Norwegian seamen who were killed in the First World War. It was named St Olav's after the first Christian King of Norway in the eleventh century. St Olaf came to the aid of King Ethelred the Unready in the Battle of London Bridge against the Danes in 1014. There has been a church dedicated to him in the City of London since soon after his death in 1030. The Rotherhithe church named after St Olaf has a distinctive copper spire and is built of red brick. The church, built to cater for the spiritual needs of sailors bringing timber to the Surrey Docks, has a barrel-vaulted roof made from timber and walls lined with oak. The weathervane on top of the spire is shaped like a Viking long boat. This was damaged by a drifting barrage balloon during the Second World War. The church achieved national press publicity in 1940 after Hitler's forces invaded Norway. While the pastor was praying for Norway on 10 April 1940, another Norwegian on the short-wave radio was telling the world about the bombing of his country. There is no longer an average evening congregation of one hundred sailors a day but the church provides a busy centre for the Norwegian community in London. The church is visited by the King of Norway once a year.

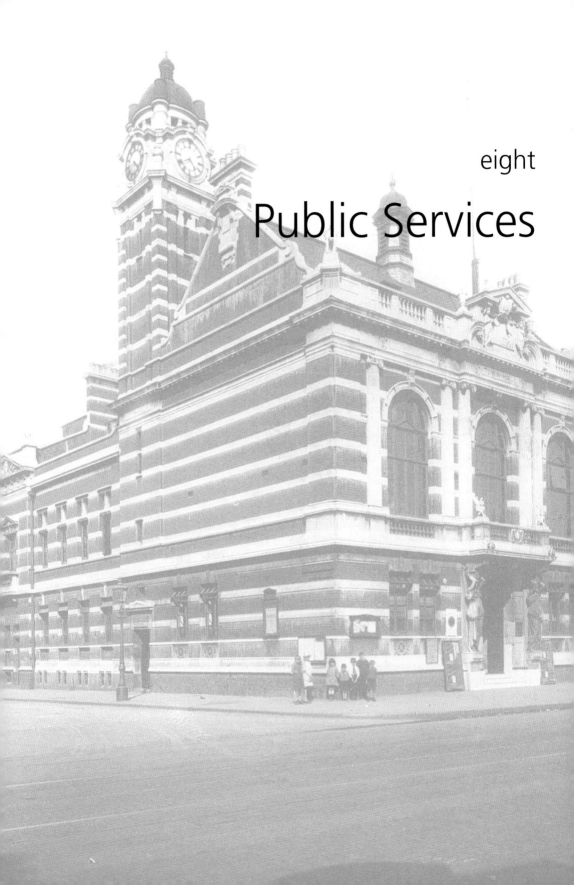

eight

Public Services

A police station occupied the site at the corner of Camberwell Green and Camberwell New Road, where the Camberwell Green Surgery is today. It was opened in 1820 and added to by the leasing of the neighbouring houses in 1829 and 1857. In Police Orders dated 11 January 1864 Camberwell Police Station was designated 'P' Division. The staff was shown as two sergeants and five constables. *The Official Encyclopaedia of Scotland Yard* by Martin Fido and Keith Skinner records that during the 1872 police strike the Camberwell sergeants and men refused to go on duty during the night of 16 November. Consideration was given in 1893 to building a new police station. A freehold site was purchased the following year at No. 22 Church Street for £4,000. The land had been owned by the Metropolitan Board of Works. The *South London Observer and Camberwell and Peckham Times* reported on 15 June 1898: 'With a modesty characteristic of "the force", the new police station in Church Street, Camberwell, was opened without any imposing ceremonial on Monday by Inspector Fox and his men. The usefulness of the new building was clearly demonstrated on Saturday, when the guardians of the peace were merely "moving in", as their first prisoner was an un-muzzled dog, which rushed in at the temporarily open door, and claimed the honour of being first "run in"'. The local newspaper, which was later taken over by the *South London Press* stated: 'The old hideous station at Camberwell Green has already been sold, and will be removed to make way, probably, for a station (Camberwell) on the proposed branch on the City and South London Electric Railway to Camberwell, Peckham and Dulwich. The new police station has accommodation for married and single officers, and is fitted with all the latest improvements'.

Right: *A fire engine races away from Dulwich Fire Station, c. 1906.*

Opposite: *The original Camberwell Police Station is seen here, c. 1890.*

Next to Fireman's Alley in Lordship Lane stands a telephone exchange that was opened on 2 May 1962. It was named Townley to commemorate Margaret Townley, the mother of Edward Alleyn who founded Dulwich College. The natural choice of name for the new telephone exchange was Dulwich, but because of the sequence of the letters in the old dialling system, DUL was the same as FUL which was the dialling code for Fulham. The telephone exchange was built on the site of Dulwich Fire Station, which was opened on 31 July 1893 by Commissary-General Downes, chairman of the Fire Brigade Committee of the London County Council. It accommodated one officer, nine firemen (all married men), one coachman and four horses. The appliances comprised one steamer, one manual engine, hose and four fire escapes. It took twenty-five seconds from an alarm being raised to the departure of the appliance. The first call of the newly-opened station was at 2.40 a.m. following the opening, to a fire at St John's Villas, Goose Green. The *South London Press* reported the opening ceremony on Saturday 5 August 1893 and began: 'At last Dulwich has its long-looked-for and much-needed fire station. It has been constructed contiguous to the Lordship Lane entrance to Dulwich Park, and facing Adon Mount, the residence of Mr James Henderson. The site has been leased from the Dulwich College Estates Governors – the County Council as yet having no compulsory powers to acquire a freehold. Upon it there has been reared a not un-picturesque structure in red brick, with stone facings, from whose beacon-like "look out" it is possible to command an extensive view of the surrounding territory'. The fire station was severely damaged during the Second World War. It was closed in 1947 and demolished in 1958.

The old police station in Peckham's High Street is being demolished.

HRH The Princess Alexandra reopened Peckham Police Station in 1988 after it had been extended. In Peckham High Street stands the building that was opened in 1893 and photographs exist of the original police station that stood on that site. The building was known as The Clock House because it had a four-faced clock on top. It was leased in 1847 from Henry Thomas Perkins to be used for police purposes. It had previously been occupied by the wealthy Dalton family. It was formerly part of their fine mansion and was subsequently used as a nunnery. In 1844 Camberwell Vestry, which ran civic affairs in the parish of Camberwell which included Peckham, contributed £3,831 19s to the police. Its contribution in 1873 amounted to £14,009 1s 5d, an increase of over 265 per cent. In *Ye Parish of Camerwell*, published in 1875, W.H. Blanch wrote a few pages on lighting and watching in which he provided information on crime. In 1816 it was stated that 'burglaries and robberies have of late increased in this parish to an alarming extent'. The Camberwell Vestry recorded that more effective measures were needed 'to secure the lives and properties of its inhabitants during the ensuing winter'. Two Acts of Parliament had been obtained, one in 1776 and the other in 1787, for 'Lighting and Watching the villages of Camberwell and Peckham, and certain roads leading thereto; and for establishing a foot patrol between Peckham and Blackman Street in the Borough of Southwark'. The Peckham Trust for watchmen met at The Red Bull in the High Street. The patrols had to go and return every half hour from The Red Bull to the Green Man turnpike in the Kent Road.

Rotherhithe Town Hall was an impressive building during the early 1930s.

Rotherhithe had its own impressive Town Hall which opened on 28 April 1897. This was only three years before Rotherhithe Vestry ceased being the body that ran local affairs. The Vestry had previously met in the Baths and Wash Houses building where Seven Islands Leisure Centre is today. Rotherhithe Town Hall, which included a library from 1905, was in Lower Road opposite St Olave's Hospital. 'When are we going to get our town hall finished?' was the predominant question asked at a meeting in 1896 of the Rotherhithe Vestry. The chairman replied: 'We've had a lot of trouble over this building. There have been nothing but delays and strikes from the commencement.' He went on: 'First of all, the builder couldn't get any stone; then he couldn't get any wood; then when he did get the materials there was a strike'. The opening ceremony, in the absence of members of the Royal Family who were too busy to attend, was performed by Mrs Carr-Gomm, the Lady of the Manor who had laid the foundation stone on 17 September 1895. A guard of honour was provided by the 3rd Volunteer Battalion of the Royal West Surrey Regiment. The band of the regiment played in the public hall (with 891 seats) where the inauguration ceremony took place after Mrs Carr-Gomm and her entourage had inspected the offices, council chamber and coroner's court. The estimated cost of the building was £15,000; the site cost £3,500. Sadly, the town hall was destroyed by bombing during the Second World War. It was probably the grandest building ever erected in the district.

Newington Public Baths featured on this postcard, c. 1910.

The impressive Newington Baths and Wash Houses in Manor Place were opened on 26 March 1898 and were in use until 1978. During the opening ceremony Canon Palmer, Rector of Newington and the oldest member of Newington Vestry that ran local affairs in the nineteenth century, declared: 'It is said that while a magnificent building like this would be very well in Paddington or Kensington, it is too large for the parish of Newington. But those who say that forget that we have a population here of 121,000 inhabitants crowded into a square mile or so of area. – no building could be too magnificent or too large for such a vast number of people'. Lord Reay, chairman of the London School Board, said: 'The children do not always come as cleanly dressed as they should at school. The difficulties are that there is no place for washing the clothes, but after this splendid palace is opened no one in Newington will be justified in sending his child to school who is not neatly attired'. James Bailey, MP said: 'It is indeed to me a great pleasure to be here today at the inauguration of these magnificent baths, which cannot but add to the comfort and welfare of the people of this vast district'. By 1936 improvements were made to the system for cleaning the water in the swimming bath. A new continuous filtration, operating on a two-and-a-half hour turnover, was introduced. This had the most modern method known – Vosmaer Perfect System of Electrolytic Ozonation. Manor Place Baths were the first in Britain to use this ozonation plant.

Grove Vale Depot was opened in 1901 when Alderman Matthew Wallace was the Mayor of Camberwell.

G rove Vale Depot, close to East Dulwich Station, was demolished and housing built on the site. The land where Besant Place and Hayes Grove were built was part of Plagquett Hall Farm in the eighteenth century. When Camberwell Borough Council was established in 1900, a depot was needed for its horses and vehicles so one was built on vacant land at the rear of shops in Grove Vale. The depot was opened by the first Mayor of Camberwell, Cllr Matthew Wallace, on 21 October 1901. The contract for the entire work amounted to £28,195. An additional sum of £2,000 was spent on machinery. The *South London Press* reported the proceedings five days later and referred to the 'fine range of buildings' that was designed by the Borough Engineer, William Oxtoby. All the corn and fodder for the council's horses, which pulled the carts at the beginning of the twentieth century, was kept in the depot. The council's carpenters, wheelwrights, farriers, smiths, painters and other mechanics were based there. Repairs to rolling stock were carried out as well as the shoeing of horses that were stabled there. The buildings included a veterinary surgeon's room. The horses 'gaudily beribboned by their drivers' were paraded prior to the opening ceremony. In his speech, the mayor said that the ratepayers demanded that the roads should be properly cleaned, the dust removed in the middle of the night and that no paper or garbage be seen on Sunday mornings. The councillors believed that neither their men nor their horses should work more than six days a week. The opening ceremony ended with a band playing God Save the King. A Borough of Camberwell Souvenir of the Opening of Grove Vale Depot and a remarkable collection of photographs, plans, newspaper cuttings and other documents relating to this celebration can be seen in Southwark Local Studies Library.

The North Camberwell Baths, also known as the Old Kent Road Baths, were the first public baths in London to have a Turkish bath. The building, which stood at the corner of Marlborough Road (now Grove), was opened by the Mayor of Camberwell, Cllr J.R. Tomkins, on Thursday 19 October 1905. He said that bathing was the healthiest, happiest, jolliest recreation that could be found. The *South London Press* on Saturday 21 October stated that at the opening ceremony the majority of the aldermen and councillors were in 'faultless evening dress'. The site was acquired by Camberwell Vestry (the forerunner of Camberwell Council) in 1898. Fifty-two competitive sets of plans were submitted. The building, which cost about £55,000, was designed by Mr E. Harding Payne. There were two swimming baths (first and second class) each with a water area of 75ft by 30ft. In addition the building had thirty men's first class warm baths, twelve second class with one rain douche and spray bath. For women there were eight first-class and eight second-class slipper baths and six rain douche baths. A Russian vapour bath accommodated nine people at one time; this was for second-class bathers. The Turkish bath, for first-class bathers, accommodated fourteen people at one time. The public wash house provided accommodation for forty-six washers. Tanks to store 60,000 gallons of cold water were situated over the wash house. A well was sunk to provide water. It provided 12,000 to 15,000 gallons per hour. These baths were completely destroyed during the Second World War. They are shown on *Old Ordnance Survey Maps: Old Kent Road 1914* (Godfrey Edition). A photograph of the stonelaying ceremony, a souvenir brochure and a programme for the opening ceremony can be seen in Southwark Local Studies Library.

Above: *Carter Street Police Station was photographed in August 1931.*

Opposite: *The Old Kent Road Baths were an important facility before the Second World War.*

Walworth Police Station in Manor Place opened in December 1993. It cost over £4 million and replaced the now derelict building in Carter Place. The origins of the old police station date back to 1856 when the lease on a house and grounds known as Walworth House was bought for a police station in Walworth Road. The station was known as Walworth/Carter Street and accommodated one inspector and thirty single constables. In 1861 the leasehold interest of land at the rear of the building was sold to the London, Chatham and Dover Railway for the building of a railway viaduct on the condition that the arches could be used by the police. In 1875 the Receiver for the Metropolitan Police District purchased the freehold of the remainder of the lease for £3,710. The police station was demolished in 1909 and the Carter Street station was built and opened in 1910 to serve the growing needs of the district. In 1950 the part of Carter Street in which the station was based was renamed Carter Place so the Commissioner of the Metropolitan Police was requested to change the name of the station to Walworth but he refused. Carter Street Police Station became a sub-divisional station of M Division with Camberwell as its Sectional Station in 1965, when new local authority and police boundaries were introduced. Officers who served at Carter Street have recalled its macho reputation in dealing with South London criminals, including the Richardson gang, who were held in the cells. The Great Train Robbers were also among the local clientele, who were also known to serving officers. A former police officer who served at Carter Street Police Station for thirty years, *South London Press* columnist Harry Cole, has written a number of amusing books about his experiences.

Peckham's first two fire stations could still be seen in 1979.

Horses for the fire engine of the Surrey Volunteer Fire Brigade in Hill Street, Peckham, were provided in 1864 by Thomas Tilling whose grave can be seen in Nunhead Cemetery. Peckham's first fire station opened in 1867; the building still exists in Peckham Road. This is a few metres from the present one which was opened on 2 March 1991 by Cllr A.G. King, Chair of the London Fire and Civil Defence Authority, and Cllr Tony Richie who was the Southwark member of the authority. The present fire station occupies the site of one which the London County Council had built. This was opened on 9 July 1925 by Geoffrey Head, chairman of the LCC Fire Brigade Committee. The *South London Press* reported that it was the first of its kind in London as it was built to meet the requirements of the shift system. The newspaper stated: 'The reason for the change is that the men nowadays live in their own homes and are only at the station during their period of duty. The only residential quarters provided are those for the station officer, although there are a mess room and a recreation room with other accommodation for the shift men. At the rear is a large drill yard with the best drill tower in London'. *Transport in Peckham and Nunhead* includes a picture of Thomas Tilling's grave and a map of how to find it. The book also shows a horse-drawn fire engine used by the London Fire Brigade. The last occasion on which a steam fire engine was used in the County of London was on 23 December 1917 in Southampton Street (now Way), close to the Peckham Fire Station.

Few cars ran past Bermondsey's Public Health Centre when this photograph was taken.

The former Public Health Centre run by the Metropolitan Borough of Bermondsey still stands in Grange Road. It was opened on 7 November 1936 by the mayor (Cllr G. Loveland). A souvenir of the event is in Southwark Local Studies Library. The *Children's Newspaper* wrote about the centre a few months before it opened and stated: 'We believe it is the first central municipal clinic in England'. Before the Second World War, Dr Alfred Salter and Bermondsey Borough Council succeeded in improving the health of local people when Britain's first municipal solarium was set up in Bermondsey. The council bought a house in Grange Road and installed equipment for treatment by artificial sunlight. Doctors were invited to send along not only patients suffering from tuberculosis but those who seemed likely to get it. The sunshine of the Mediterranean was brought to the slums of Bermondsey. The solarium was moved to the new public health centre which had a variety of facilities including foot clinics. These were first established in 1930 to provide treatment for people suffering from corns, bunions, warts, callosities, in-growing toenails and other maladies of the feet. As the great majority of the inhabitants of the borough were manual workers, who were on their feet all day, the clinics became extraordinarily popular. Bermondsey was the first borough in the country to run a municipal foot clinic. The new public health centre also included infant welfare clinics, ante-natal clinics, gynaecological clinics, a tuberculosis centre, an electro-medical department, a dental clinic, an X-ray department and a laboratory for the public analyst. For fourteen years prior to the centre being built, Bermondsey Borough Council achieved a considerable measure of fame as a pioneer in many branches of public health. Health education was also an important part of Bermondsey Council's work.

Not one vehicle could be seen when this picture of municipal buildings in Walworth Road was taken.

Three important civic buildings stand next to each other in Walworth Road – the former Newington Vestry Hall, Newington Library (which includes Cuming Museum) and the former Metropolitan Borough of Southwark Public Health Services Department at the corner of Larcom Street. The foundation stone for the latter, the newest of the three buildings, was laid on 11 July 1936 by the Mayor of Southwark, Cllr T.G. Gibbings. The Health Services Department was opened on 25 September 1937 by the next mayor, Cllr C.J. Mills. In the official programme the chairman of the Public Health and Sanitary Committee, Cllr Arthur J. Gillian, wrote: 'It would be a mistake for anyone to conclude that the completion of the new Department denotes the end of the Borough Council's efforts; on the contrary, the opening ceremony marks a further great step towards the Council's goal, which is the betterment of the health of the people of Southwark generally... The Council took the view that when the health of the people, and particularly the poorer classes of our population, is involved, only the best equipment and the most modern scientific devices would suffice. It was for that reason that the Council undertook the erection of the new department'. During the opening ceremony Cllr Gillian described the centre as a great effort to track down and fight the menace of diseases. The *South London Press* reported that the new building included a tuberculosis centre, dental and sanitary services, an artificial and radiant heat clinic, a maternity and child welfare centre, a solarium and a Public Analyst's Department. Brochures to mark the stone laying and opening of the Health Services Department can be seen in Southwark Local Studies Library. The building is included in *The Story of Walworth* by Mary Boast.

The grounds of Honor Oak Crematorium were deserted when a photographer snapped this view.

Honor Oak Crematorium was opened by the prominent physician Lord Horder on 29 March 1939. Towards the end of the nineteenth century, Camberwell Vestry, the forerunner of Camberwell Borough Council, considered providing a crematorium. However, it was about forty years later that the council realised the importance of cremation as a means of disposal for dead people. So the council used its power under the Cremation Act 1902 to build a crematorium. Before this could be done, a public inquiry was held at Camberwell Town Hall by one of the inspectors from the Ministry of Health. The inquiry was into the application of Camberwell Borough Council for consent to borrow £20,745 for the provision of a crematorium and garden of remembrance on a site forming part of the land acquired for use as a burial ground at Honor Oak, and for approval of the plans and site of the crematorium. Two Lewisham ratepayers were present at the inquiry in 1937. One appeared on behalf of residents of Honor Oak Park who opposed the scheme. He asked whether it would be better to remove burial grounds out of London and into the country. A representative from Camberwell Borough Council said that in 1901 the council had acquired a very large area of land comprising sixty-seven-and-a-half acres at Honor Oak Park on which there was an outstanding debt of £12,605. There were 2,500 interments a year in the burial grounds of the Council. The representative said that the time would come when that method of disposal of dead people of ordinary means would be out of the question. A photograph of Honor Oak Crematorium soon after it was opened is included in *The Story of Peckham and Nunhead* published by Southwark Local Studies Library.

The interior of the Kirkwood Training Centre is seen here in 1954.

A civil defence training centre stood in Peckham at the corner of Kirkwood Road and Brayards Road. Housing now occupies the site. Kirkwood Training Centre was opened by a former Home Secretary, Mr Chuter Ede, on 9 October 1954. The building was self-contained. It had administration and equipment rooms, a large kitchen and servery. The main hall was equipped for lectures and demonstrations. It had ultra-violet light for technical studies and a 20ft square floor map of Camberwell. The Training Centre included a stage for Civil Defence playlets and social activities as well as a film screen. Gas and fire training huts were provided in the grounds. A civil defence officer, Mr L.J. Hall, said: 'Everything possible to attract recruits is provided. We believe that if you are going to ask a man or woman to leave their comfortable fireside chairs to do civil defence work you must give equal comfort at the training centre'. Before Mr Chuter Ede opened the Kirkwood Training Centre, on the same day he went to Camberwell's new Civil Defence headquarters and control centre in Peckham Road, at the corner of Vestry Road. This was an underground building which was the best of its kind in London. On the day before the former Home Secretary's visit to Camberwell and Peckham, the *South London Press* wrote an editorial which began: 'Of every pound the government raises in taxes now 7s. 4d. is spent in "defence". Add to that 2s 8d paid as interest on war loan and national savings and, one way or another, exactly 10s has gone or is going on war preparations but Civil Defence still has to be done mainly by the great unpaid'.

nine

Recreation

Engravings were made of Hogarth's painting of Southwark Fair.

The Crown in 1460 granted the City of London permission to hold a fair in Southwark. From its earliest days it was a boisterous event, which initially lasted for three days but was later extended to a fortnight. It was held in September at the southern end of what today is Borough High Street. As with other English fairs, a market that was created for the sale of livestock, cheese, corn and cloth gradually became a place of entertainment featuring wild beasts, bear-baiting and other attractions. The fair's heyday was in the eighteenth century but as a result of the congestion it caused, Southwark Fair was closed in 1756. The famous artist William Hogarth (1697-1764) painted Southwark Fair in 1733. It was acquired just a century later by the fourth Duke of Newcastle when he bought the Johnes Hafod estates, with the literary and art possessions, at the lock-stock-and-barrel price of £70,000. The painting was sold at Christie's in 1937 and is now in the Cincinnati Art Museum in the American state of Ohio. The writer Charles Lamb said that, 'Hogarth's pictures were full of words'. The painter possessed the masterly gift of weaving a web of detail into his work. In his painting called Southwark Fair, Hogarth showed all the fun of the fair which was enjoyed with gusto by the robust and jolly folk of his day. In the centre of the picture is the old St George the Martyr church. Hogarth set about his task to portray all the celebrated public figures composing the crowd. In the centre is the theatrical heroine drumming up the crowd for a performance of the *Siege of Troy* by Elkanah Settle. Southwark Fair, including William Hogarth's print, is included in *Southwark: An Illustrated Guide* by Leonard Reilly published by Southwark Local Studies Library.

The excavated remains of the Rose Theatre in Park Street were photographed from Southwark Bridge Road by archivist and author Stephen Humphrey on 14 May 1989.

The remains of the sixteenth-century Rose Theatre were discovered in 1989 when archaeologists from the Museum of London investigated a site in north Southwark. The excavation began as a routine operation, which was planned to take place during the interval between one office being demolished and another being built. Soon the archaeologists realised that they had found the site of one of the great playhouses of Elizabethan England. They had discovered the Rose Theatre, which was built in 1587 and where plays written by Shakespeare, Marlowe, Jonson and Kyd were performed. The theatre's remains were due to be destroyed by the foundations of a new office block but actors, scholars and the general public joined together to save this remarkable fragment of theatre history for future generations. Suddenly, the archaeologists found themselves at the centre of an international media frenzy. The atmosphere on the site veered between a street carnival and a memorial service as the long hot summer of 1989 wore on. Thousands of people came to take what they thought might be their last chance to view the theatre's remains. The plans for the new office block went ahead but its foundations were altered to avoid damaging the theatre remains. These were isolated within a separate basement space so that they can be put on display to the public if sufficient money can be raised to do the necessary work. An exciting light and sound presentation on this major archaeological site brings to life the story of the Rose Theatre.

A replica of the Globe Theatre stands close to the site of the original one.

Actress Zoë Wanamaker proudly received a blue plaque at the South London Gallery in 2003 to commemorate her father's tireless efforts in enabling a replica of Shakespeare's theatre, the Globe, to be built in Southwark. The Globe stood just south of modern Park Street, just east of where it runs underneath Southwark Bridge Road. It was part-owned by William Shakespeare. The Globe was erected in 1599 using wood from a Shoreditch theatre called the Theatre. Unfortunately the Globe was destroyed by fire in 1613. The thatched roof was set alight by a cannon ball fired during a performance of Shakespeare's *Henry VIII*. The theatre was rebuilt the following year. Many of Shakespeare's plays had their first public performances at the Globe including *Hamlet, Othello, Macbeth* and *King Lear*. American actor Sam Wanamaker was very keen to see a replica of the Globe built in Southwark. When as a young man he toured the streets of Bankside and the Borough he was shocked to find that there was insufficient commemoration of William Shakespeare's original theatre and that there was virtually no recognition of the playwright himself. When he was at the peak of his theatrical career, Sam Wanamaker decided to devote the remainder of his life to correcting this wrong. He bought a house in Falmouth Road, SE1, and began to bully, harry and hassle not only Southwark Council but individuals and firms around the world. After a long, difficult and frustrating campaign, the new Globe was finally opened in 1994. Tragically, Sam Wanamaker had died the previous year. Sam Wanamaker is included in *Southwark: Who Was Who* by Shirley Harrison and Sally Evemy. The Globe is in *The Story of Bankside* by Leonard Reilly and Geoff Marshall.

Surrey Theatre was one of the most successful popular theatres in London.

The obelisk at St George's Circus can be seen in the above 1812 drawing. The large building on the left became the Surrey Theatre. The Circus was laid out as a road junction after the first Blackfriars Bridge was opened in 1769. Tolls were collected to pay for a new road leading to the bridge and for its upkeep. Nearby in 1782 a trick horse rider called Charles Hughes and song-writer Charles Dibdin established the Royal Circus and Equestrian Philharmonic Academy. Unfortunately, it was burned down in 1803. Two years later it was rebuilt and drunken, eccentric actor-manager Robert Elliston became the proprietor in 1809. He blatantly evaded the Patent Act (which strictly limited the number of theatres which could produce plays) by inserting a ballet into every play including *Hamlet* and *Macbeth*. The building was renamed the Surrey Theatre in 1816; it was one of London's most successful popular theatres. After another fire, it was rebuilt again in 1865. A wide variety of plays were performed – Shakespeare, adaptations of Dickens, melodrama and pantomime. The Surrey Theatre was the most famous and longest surviving of many nineteenth century theatres and music halls in what today is the London Borough of Southwark. Productions continued until 1921 when the Surrey Theatre became a cinema, which lasted only until 1923. It was demolished in 1935 and an extension to the Royal Eye Hospital was built on the site. The Surrey Theatre is included in *The Story of Bankside* by Leonard Reilly and Geoff Marshall and *Southwark Past* by Richard Tames. It is marked on *Old Ordnance Survey Maps: Waterloo & Southwark 1872*. All can be obtained from Southwark Local Studies Library which also has many early playbills and programmes of the Surrey Theatre.

Stephen Lawrence House and other new housing in Southampton Way stand where the Rosemary Branch Tavern and its extensive grounds used to be in the nineteenth century. In *Ye Parish of Camerwell* (published in 1875) W.H. Blanch wrote: 'The Rosemary Branch, Peckham, although possessing but a local reputation at the present time, was a well-known metropolitan hostelrie half a century ago'. The old house had rustic surroundings. Tradition has it that whenever the landlord of the old house tapped a barrel of beer, the inhabitants for some distance around were made aware of it by the ringing of a bell and a proclamation. When the new public house was built, it was described in a print of the time as an 'establishment which had no suburban rival'. The grounds surrounding it were most extensive. Horse racing, cricket, pigeon shooting and all kinds of outdoor sports and pastimes were carried on. The first recorded balloon ascent in Peckham took place on 7 April 1847 when Lt George Burcher Gale, RN ascended in a gas balloon with a Mr Byrne from the grounds of the Rosemary Branch Tavern. 'Persons of scientific character' had been invited to attend. The balloon contained 34,000 cubit feet of coal gas supplied by the Metropolitan Gas Co. By 1875 the grounds had been almost entirely covered with houses. Only one small field remained and even that was being laid out ready to be built on. In the 1890s the Rosemary Branch was a popular music hall known as Peckham Theatre of Varieties. The Rosemary Branch and lots of other pubs are included in a book by Ron Woollacott called *Nunhead & Peckham Pubs Past and Present: A pub crawl through time*.

Right: *The Elephant and Castle Theatre was photographed in this image, c. 1907.*

Opposite: *Peckham was in Surrey when this view was drawn.*

The former Coronet Cinema in New Kent Road, which closed in 1999, is now a live music venue. The cinema building opened on 31 May 1879 as the Elephant and Castle Theatre, with seating capacity of 2,203 on the site of an earlier theatre which burnt down on 26 March 1878. The original theatre had opened in 1872. It was erected as a public hall but was never completed. Instead, it was converted into a theatre. At the end of the last performance before the theatre closed in 1928, members of the Jack Sheppard Company and the audience joined hands in singing *Auld Lang Syne* and *Knocked 'em in the Old Kent Road*. An article about the closure of the theatre, published in 1928, shows a picture of it with a model elephant with a castle on its back above the entrance. Another picture is included in *Southwark, Bermondsey and Rotherhithe in Old Photographs* by Stephen Humphrey. This out-of-print book and the article can be seen in Southwark Local Studies Library. Next to the theatre stood the two old houses which still stand beside the former Coronet Cinema. The theatre was converted into the Elephant and Castle Cinema that opened in 1931 with 2,315 seats. After modernisation it became the ABC on 9 October 1967 with *Bonny and Clyde*. The ABC closed on 25 January 1981 with *Times Square*. It then reopened on 7 May with *Funhouse* and *My Bloody Valentine* in the 648-seat Screen 1, *Ordinary People* in 286-seat Screen 2, and *Elephant Man* in 220-seat Screen 3. The ABC became the Coronet in 1987.

The Empire, seen here in 1907, was a prominent feature at the corner of Denmark Hill and Coldharbour Lane.

A theatre and then a cinema occupied land in Denmark Hill where The Camberwell Foyer and Nando's restaurant are today, at the corner of Coldharbour Lane. The *South London Press* on 27 October 1894 showed a drawing of the Theatre Metropole and stated: 'We are pleased to announce that this new and magnificent theatre will positively open on Monday next, October 29.' The LCC had inspected the building and 'found everything in a highly satisfactory condition'. It was a high-class theatre for plays and opera. The proprietor was Mr J.B. Mulholland who aimed to bring West End successes to Camberwell. The theatre had a very ornate interior with private boxes, stalls, dress circle, balcony and gallery. Ladies who went to the theatre wearing fashionable hats 'were respectfully informed that hats and bonnets are not allowed in the stalls or first two rows of the dress circle'. Drawings of the interior of the Theatre Metropole were included in an article on the life of Camberwell by H.D. Lowry published in an 1895 edition of *The Windsor Magazine*. This can be found in Southwark Local Studies Library. The theatre's name was later changed to the Empire and a picture of it appeared in the *South London Press* on 10 August 1937 with the announcement that it was to be demolished to make way for a new Odeon cinema. The Odeon had a seating capacity of 2,470. It opened on 20 March 1939 with *Men With Wings*. The last film shown before the cinema closed on 5 July 1975 was *The Night Porter*. The cinema then became a Dickie Dirts clothing warehouse. The Theatre Metropole is included in *The Story of Camberwell* by Mary Boast.

The Oriental Palace of Varieties was built in Camberwell in 1896, at the corner of Denmark Hill and Orpheus Street, by a company under the famous comedian Dan Leno. Three years later it was rebuilt as the Camberwell Palace of Varieties with seating for about 3,000 people. The *South London Press* included drawings of the music hall on 4 November 1899. This temple of amusement was opened on Monday 20 November 1899. The enthusiastic audience packed the entire seating space and overflowed into gangways and corners. The building was erected from the design of Mr E.A.E. Woodrow by Mr C. Gray Hill of Coventry, who built the Shakespeare Theatre at Clapham and other modern theatres. Under the somewhat hurried conditions of opening the first show, it was inevitable that some hitches would occur regarding the seating accommodation. For about half-an-hour the acting manager and his henchman were busy smoothing the ruffled feelings of disappointed visitors and devising means of putting the proverbial quart into a pint pot. When the curtain rose a soloist and choir sang the National Anthem. The vast audience then settled down in the best of humours to the entertainment. A roar of applause greeted the entrance of Mr Herbert Campbell, which then subsided into sympathetic murmurs when that burly comedian expressed his deep sorrow at not being able to perform as neither his costume nor his music had arrived. By way of penance he promised to send five guineas to the Widows and Orphans Fund. The Camberwell Palace closed in 1956. *The Story of Camberwell* by Mary Boast includes the cover of a playbill produced by the Camberwell Palace of Varieties. The music hall is shown on *Old Ordnance Survey Maps: Camberwell & Stockwell 1913*.

A postcard shows the Palace of Varieties, c. 1905.

The Trocette was derelict when this photograph was taken in 1961.

Trocette Mansions in Bermondsey Street were built on the site of the Trocette cinema which opened in 1929 as the Super. This was a huge cold place that quickly won the affection of cinemagoers who nicknamed it 'The Ice-box'. The Hyams brothers bought the Super from George Smart in 1933 and renamed it the Trocette. Phil, Sid and Mick Hyams, the sons of an East End baker, once dubbed the 'three wise men of the Yeast' by Fleet Street journalist Hannen Swaffer, did a swift revamp job on the Super. They had a very efficient heating system installed which encouraged patrons to change its name to 'The Bake'. The vast 2,282 seat auditorium was to a large extent belied by the modest foyer and facade of the cinema which shared the same amount of pavement as the Horse Shoe pub next door. Victor McLaglen, star of British silent films, judged a beauty contest at the Trocette in 1933. He won the hearts of many Bermondsey girls that day by describing the winners as the most beautiful girls he had ever seen. 'They dress neatly, talk quietly and most important of all are not artificial', he said. In its early days the Trocette was taking over £400 a week and the Hyams managed to sell out to Gaumont British in 1944 before the rot set in. A former cinema manager, Maurice Cheepen, said: 'The yobs used to take exit doors off their hinges and sling bricks through the office windows. It was a tough place.' He remembered 'throwing out' one of Bermondsey's most celebrated boys on a number of occasions – Tommy Steele, whom he described as 'a little terror'. The cinema closed on 7 January 1956 with *Touch and Go* and *Veils of Baghdad*.

The Trocadero was photographed in 1931, the year after it had opened.

The Trocadero cinema in the New Kent Road opened on 22 December 1930. It had a seating capacity of 3,394 and was one of the largest cinemas in Europe. The *South London Press* reported the opening by stating: 'The new Trocadero Cinema at Elephant and Castle will go down to theatrical history as the Theatre That Opened in a Fog. There were extraordinary scenes – so far as anything could be seen – outside the building at the opening on Monday night. Huge crowds who had waited from early afternoon for seats were joined in the evening by thousands waiting for trams, which were almost at a standstill owing to the fog'. Special patrols of police who had been detailed to handle the crowds outside the building had to spend their time keeping the roads clear for the traffic which could only dimly be seen. Music, played by the band inside the cinema, attracted more people, and a few thousand other sightseers came to see what the crowd was about. The result was a dense mass of people thronging the pavements and overflowing into the roads, whilst traffic hooted and drivers shouted in an effort to get through the hold-up. At 8 o'clock, a quarter of an hour before the performance began, 'House Full' boards were put out. The first film shown was *Bed and Breakfast* starring Richard Cooper and Jane Baxter, followed by *The Storm*. In *The Story of Walworth* Mary Boast wrote: 'One special feature of the "Troc" was the magnificent Wurlitzer organ, shipped from America in 1930'. The cinema closed on 19 October 1963 and was demolished but the Wurlitzer organ was transferred by the Cinema Organ Society to what is now London South Bank University.

Seen here in 1979, the former Gaumont cinema became a bingo hall in 1961.

The former Gaumont cinema in Peckham High Street was demolished so Gaumont House could be built on the site. It took an army of men ten months to build the cinema and 650 tons of steelwork were used – all of British design and manufacture. The auditorium had seating accommodation for 2,250 with a total capacity of 2,500. The stalls had 1,350 seats with standing space for 250 more. There was one large circle with 950 seats. The Gaumont Palace, as it was originally called, opened its doors on 8 February 1932 at 1.30 p.m. Hundreds of people had waited from 11 a.m. and special police had to be called out to see that the gasping and giggling did not completely disorganise the traffic. The *South London Press* reported that over 2,000 Peckham residents attended the opening performance. 'They gasped, then giggled, and finally they settled down wonderingly to drink in the delights of the new magnificence that had invaded the High Street.' The Mayor of Camberwell, Alderman Arthur Pearman, expressed his great pleasure in officially opening the Palace which he believed was a great acquisition for Peckham, the ratepayers and the shopkeepers in the High Street. Mr H.W. Froude, Gaumont's local area inspector, told the audience that the site on which the cinema stood was one of the first purchases made by his company who had made it their policy that 'nothing but the best was good enough for Peckham'. The souvenir brochure can be seen in Southwark Local Studies Library and includes the opening programme. The first film shown was a humorous talkie *A Fowl Affair*. After Ideal Cinemagazine and British Movietone News came *Almost a Divorce*. Then followed *The Calendar* by Edgar Wallace who went to school in Peckham. There was also stage entertainment. The Gaumont Palace was built on the site of Crown Theatre which had opened in 1898. The cinema became the first Top Rank Bingo Club in 1961 and closed in 1998.

ten

Street Scene

The obelisk was decorated for Queen Victoria's diamond jubilee procession on 22 June 1897.

An Obelisk that stood near the Imperial War Museum was moved in 1998 back to its original site in St George's Circus. In 1769 an Act was passed enabling the City Corporation to build Blackfriars Road. After the road was completed, the corporation ordered the surveyor to prepare 'a drawing of an Obelisk, to be erected in the middle of the Circus in St George's Fields, to serve as a milestone and to which lamps may be affixed'. The structure was finished during 1771 and the following inscriptions were included:

> North side – One mile 350 feet from Fleet Street
> East side – One mile 40 feet from London Bridge
> West side – One mile from Palace Yard, Westminster Hall

When the Bridge House Estates Committee learnt that only three sides out of four bore an inscription, they ordered that the City Arms be engraved on the Obelisk and that reference be made to the mayoralty of Mr Brass Crosby. The Obelisk remained a local landmark until it was removed in 1905 to the grounds of Bethlem Hospital (the building which now houses the Imperial War Museum), so that a clock tower could be erected in St George's Circus. This was opened in 1907 and was a gift from William Bowland Faulkner and Frederick Faulkner who were about to sever their connection with the old Borough of Southwark after having been associated with it for over sixty years. The clock tower was demolished in 1937 and can be seen on page 2 of this book. The Obelisk is shown on the 1872 Waterloo and Southwark map in the Old Ordnance Survey Maps series published by Alan Godfrey who has produced various old maps covering the whole of what is now the London Borough of Southwark.

This Marshalsea Prison building was a short distance away from where Southwark Local Studies Library is situated today but on the same side of Borough High Street.

John Wesley, the founder of Methodism, visited Marshalsea Prison, which he described as 'a nursery of all manner of wickedness'. In his journal on 3 February 1753 he wrote: 'Oh shame to man that there should be such a place, such a picture of hell upon earth! And shame to those who bear the name of Christ that there should need any prison at all in Christendom!' Marshalsea Prison occupied various sites along Borough High Street until it was closed in 1842. It was principally a debtors' prison, which was overcrowded partly because prisoners' children were housed with them. The prison administration by the Knight Marshal, a Crown official, was extremely corrupt. The last building to be used as Marshalsea Prison occupied the site where Southwark Local Studies Library is today. One of the prison walls separates the library from the churchyard of St George the Martyr. Charles Dickens knew Marshalsea Prison very well. Much of the first part of his story *Little Dorrit* revolves around it. In 1856 Dickens wrote: 'Thirty years ago there stood, a few doors short of the church of St George, in the Borough of Southwark, on the left-hand side of the way going southward, the Marshalsea Prison. It had stood there many years before and it remained there some years afterwards, but it is gone now and the world is none the worse without it'. The Marshalsea Prison pump can be seen in the Cuming Museum in Walworth Road. The prison is included in *The Journal of John Wesley* abridged by Christopher Idle (Lion Publishing) and *Southwark Remembered* (Tempus Publishing) as well as *Southwark: An Illustrated History* by Leonard Reilly and *Charles Dickens and Southwark* published by Southwark Council.

Spectators used boats to gain a clear view of the Great Fire of Tooley Street.

L ondon's worst fire since the Great Fire in 1666 happened in Tooley Street in 1861.
This Southwark street had many warehouses; some were packed with inflammable or
explosive goods. Fires were not unusual and some were disastrous; one on 19 August
1843 was very serious. The Great Fire of Tooley Street started around 5.00 p.m. on
Saturday 22 June 1861 in a jute and hemp store at Cotton's Wharf. This was not far from
London Bridge. The London Fire Engine Establishment could not obtain water when it
first arrived. Not even two floating fire engines could operate as the tide was too low.
The fire quickly spread to nearby warehouses that contained oil, tallow and salt-petre.
One warehouse exploded at 7.30 p.m. killing a fireman and also James Braidwood, who
had moved south from Edinburgh in 1833 to take command of the London Fire Engine
Establishment. The fire became a major attraction for Londoners. *The Illustrated Times*
wrote: 'From all quarters people came pouring on foot, in omnibus, cab, pleasure-van,
chaise, town-carts, waggons, etc. At 9-o'clock – London Bridge and the approaches
presented all the appearance of the Epsom Road on a Derby Day... On the river itself
hundreds of boats were filled with people.' It took two weeks for the fire to be brought
under control. In that time a quarter-of-a-mile, from St Olave's church (demolished in
1926-28) to Hay's Dock, was devastated. In *The Story of Bermondsey* Mary Boast refers to
James Braidwood and states: 'There is a memorial to him high up on the wall of 33
Tooley Street. Carved in stone are his fireman's helmet and axe'. *Bermondsey and
Rotherhithe Perceived* by Peter Marcan includes a picture of a fire in 1851 shown in *The
Illustrated London News* ten years before the much bigger fire.

Frank Staples and his wife had no parking problems in 1949.

A 1931 Morris Minor was the only car in Nutfield Road, East Dulwich, when the above photograph was taken in 1949 outside No. 17. The driver, Frank Staples, and his wife Gladys lived in this Victorian street long before it became packed with cars in increasingly fashionable SE22. Nutfield Road, built in 1864, is included in the seventeen-volume survey *Life and Labour of the People in London* published by Charles Booth between 1889 and 1903. The road consisted of two-storey terrace houses with a few having an extra half storey. Two families often shared a house. The occupants included carpenters and gardeners. Archdale Road was a similar road. Both were named after roads in Fermanagh in Ulster. At the Frogley Road end of Nutfield Road was a big blank wall on the outside of the first house on the east side of the road (No. 31). This was the gathering point for children of both roads. Street games were played there. Wickets were chalked on the wall for cricket and boxes were drawn for other games such as 'It', 'Relieve Oh' and 'Weak Horses'. They were rough games but fun; there were plenty of grazed knees. Frank Staples played these games in the 1920s and '30s. In those days a coal merchant called 'King's' ran a business from 31 Nutfield Road and horses were stabled there. Unusually, the numbers of the houses go consecutively on each side of the road. The last house on the east side (No. 1) was occupied by McColloch, a firm of builders which was included in the 1874 Post Office Directory and was still there when the Second World War began. Three houses opposite were bombed in the Blitz.

Yellow lines were not needed in Grove Vale in 1951.

The picture above shows an electric tram picking up passengers in Grove Vale, East Dulwich, in 1951. The No. 84 tram was en route to Peckham Rye; the terminus was at Stuart Road. Trams ceased running along Grove Vale in October 1951. On the side of the tram is an advertisement for Oakeys Emery Cloth. The longer advert is for Wisk soap powder: 'Now Super Lather!'. The tram had just travelled under the East Dulwich Railway Bridge. The station opened in 1868 and was originally called Champion Hill Station. It was renamed East Dulwich in 1888. Rickett Cockerell Co. Ltd, coal and coke merchants, occupied the site where Dulwich Garden Centre is today. Grove Vale Library was opened on 28 October 1950 and Lord Ammon, Mayor of Camberwell, made a speech. Camberwell Borough Council had difficulty in finding a suitable site and eventually decided to convert a shop. The library later expanded by taking over a shop next door. This was used for the new junior section that opened on 3 March 1956. There was excitement in Grove Vale some years before this photograph was taken. The *South London Press* reported on 11 January 1938 that the previous Sunday a horse drawing a milk cart took fright and set off at full gallop down Grove Vale heading towards Lordship Lane. A police constable rushed across the road but the terrified animal outpaced him. With the cart swaying from side to side, it went careering on. A milk rounds-man employed by another company was standing on the pavement when he saw the runaway horse approaching. As the horse and cart drew level, he flung himself at the horse's head and grasped the reins and managed to stop the horse and cart.

eleven

Thames and Transport

London Bridge was busy in around 1920.

How many people who cross London Bridge give any thought to its history? When the Romans invaded Britain in AD 43 they flung a wooden bridge across the Thames. This enabled them to move soldiers and supplies to help conquer the country beyond. As time passed, a settlement called *Londinium* grew up on the north and south banks around the bridge. A stone bridge was completed by the beginning of the thirteenth century. This was later built over by houses, shops, churches and inns. It was a spectacular sight and was regarded as one of the wonders of the world. It stood for 622 years. That historic structure disappeared when a new bridge was built. It was opened in 1831 by William IV and Queen Adelaide. The scene on the river as they came by water from Somerset House was one of extraordinary splendour. The State Barge, escorted by nearly thirty vessels, was rowed slowly past two lines of flag-bedecked and decorated barges, steamers, yachts and craft of every description, which were moored on both sides of the Thames. That bridge is now in the USA. When it was dismantled to make way for the present London Bridge, each part was carefully numbered so the bridge could be rebuilt in Lake Havasu City, Arizona. The present bridge was opened by Queen Elizabeth II in 1973. 'I am glad to report that it shows no sign of falling down,' she said. 'Far from it: it is clearly here to stay. London Bridge may not be the longest, tallest, or the widest bridge in the world; but I believe, as you do, that is the most famous.'
A fully illustrated book by Peter Jackson *London Bridge: A Visual History* has been produced and provides further information about the bridge.

Cannon Street Railway Bridge was still under construction in 1864.

Cannon Street Railway Bridge came into use on the day the new railway station in the City of London opened – 1 September 1866. Work had begun on building the bridge in 1863. It was designed by John Hawkshaw who was consulting engineer to the South Eastern Railway. The bridge has five spans of shallow plate girders on cast-iron fluted Doric piers. It was widened in 1886-93. The original bridge, 80ft wide and 706ft long, was supported on four piers. Each pier had four cast-iron columns. The bridge carried five tracks across the river; this was increased to ten in 1892. Why were the bridge and Cannon Street Station built? At first the South Eastern Railway had been content to serve the City from London Bridge Station and two proposed intermediate stations on the Charing Cross extension (at the south end of Southwark Bridge and at Blackfriars Road), but in 1860 the London, Chatham & Dover Railway, the South Eastern Railway's great rivals, were authorised to extend into the City of London as far as Ludgate Hill. Spurred by this, the SER-backed Charing Cross Co. decided to complement the West End terminus with a City station on the north bank of the Thames. The Metropolitan District Railway had not yet been built and street congestion was bad. An Act of Parliament was passed in 1861 for a station to be built in Cannon Street, just two minutes' walk from the Bank and Mansion House. *The Illustrated London News* showed a picture of the railway bridge under construction in its 4 June 1864 edition. The view is from Southwark Bridge looking east. Cannon Street Station is included in *London Suburban Railways: Charing Cross to Dartford* by Vic Mitchell and Keith Smith (Middleton Press).

Frost fairs were frequently held on the River Thames for 600 years. Feasting and drinking were much in evidence. Oxen were roasted on the ice and the first roundabout appeared. In London the Thames froze solid at least twenty-three times between 1309 and 1814. Why has it been an extremely rare event for the capital's river to freeze since then? One possible reason is that the temperature has not been low enough. During the last two frost fairs the average temperature in 1739-40 (December to February) was 31° Fahrenheit and in 1813-14 was 32.5°. In our coldest recent winter (1962-63) the average temperature was 31 5°, but the Thames showed no sign of freezing anywhere near London. The reason for the river freezing cannot be due only to the temperature. There must have been other reasons. All the frost fairs took place upstream from the old London Bridge (which was replaced in 1831 having stood for over 600 years). When London Bridge was built in stone in 1209 it had nineteen arches (by contrast, the present London Bridge has only three). In addition, each of the twenty piers had a 'starling' around it. This was a breakwater that protected each pier from the force of the water and any debris that might damage the pier. These breakwaters reduced the flow of water through the arches so the bridge structure acted almost like a dam against the flow of the water. No frost fairs were held on the Thames after a new bridge was opened in 1831. It had only five arches and that part of the river never froze again. The river did freeze in 1895 near Tower Bridge. More information is included in *Frost Fairs on the Frozen Thames* by Nicholas Reed (Lilburne Press).

A frost fair was held on the River Thames in 1683-84.

The Bricklayers Arms sidings were still being used in 1969.

People live where the Bricklayers Arms Goods Station used to be in Bermondsey until it closed in 1981 after 137 years of commercial service. Partly because of congestion at London Bridge Station, the South Eastern Railway and the London & Croydon Railway built an independent terminus near the Bricklayers Arms Inn on the Old Kent Road. The Act of Parliament for the 1.6 mile branch line to this site received the Royal Assent in July 1843. Its route followed an undeveloped wedge of low-lying meadowland, criss-crossed by drainage ditches, between the expanding industrial suburb of Bermondsey and the ribbon development of the Old Kent Road. The site of the station was between Swan Street (now Page's Walk) and Upper Grange Road (now Dunton Road). It was the nearest point of approach to the centre of London that could be reached without much demolition work being done and expensive engineering works. Few premises apart from a rope walk had to be demolished so this reduced the cost of the land. Bricklayers Arms Station opened for both passengers and goods traffic on 1 May 1844. Though it was a considerable distance from the City centre, it was promoted as the Grand West End Terminus. The station closed to all regular passengers in 1852 but it continued to be a goods station for over a hundred years. A well-illustrated and informative article is included in *London's Industrial Archaeology No 4* (Greater London Industrial Archaeological Society). The station is shown on *Old Ordnance Survey Maps: Old Kent Road 1871.*

The view from Southwark Park Station looking towards London Bridge was captured by a photographer in the 1913-14 winter. On the left is the Corbett's Lane signal box.

Three railway bridges cross Rotherhithe New Road. The one next to Corbetts Passage is close to where Southwark Park Station was until it closed on 15 March 1915. The platforms were on the South Eastern & Chatham Railway tracks only. They were in use from 1 October 1902 so the station was open for only about twelve-and-a-half years. A station named Commercial Docks had been in use near this site between 1856 and 1866. Southwark Park Station was on the line from Charing Cross to Dartford via Greenwich. The London and Greenwich Railway's Act, passed in 1833, authorised London's first railway. The entire double track route was built on a series of 878 brick arches. This amazing engineering feat involved laying bricks at the rate of 100,000 a day. They were produced near Sittingbourne and taken by barge to a wharf on the Surrey Canal. The line came into operation between Deptford and Spa Road in February 1836. The service was extended to London Bridge in December of that year. One of the unusual features of the Act was that individual parishes were able to specify what materials had to be used for the construction of bridges over streets in their area. Another clause allowed the railway to construct a toll path beside their viaduct. This was to prove a valuable source of revenue even though the charge was only one penny per person. Southwark Park Station is included in *London Suburban Railways: Charing Cross to Dartford* by Vic Mitchell and Keith Smith (Middleton Press) and the station is shown on *Old Ordnance Survey Maps: Deptford (North) 1914* (Alan Godfrey Ltd).

Peckham Bus Garage was busy in 1979.

The bus garage was a prominent feature in Peckham High Street where the bus station is today. It was built where omnibus operator Thomas Tilling had premises in Bull Yard. He first leased them in 1876 and in 1905 adapted them as a garage for 35 buses. The company was granted a licence to construct four tanks with a total petrol capacity of 1,000 gallons. This is said to be the first example of bulk storage for a bus company; petrol was usually stored in 2-gallon cans. From 1911 Bull Yard became the engineering headquarters where Tilling petrol-electric buses were assembled and maintained. At times bus bodies were also built there. The depot was bombed in 1940. Fire destroyed the premises and forty-eight vehicles parked there. The Peckham Bus Garage was built on the site. This opened in 1951 and was London Transport's first post-war garage. The 52,800 square feet parking area was roofed in reinforced concrete to the latest 'barrel' design. This was the first of its kind in London. The garage was designed by Wallis Gilbert and Partners who were also architects for the Firestone building in Brentford and the Hoover Building at Perivale. The London Transport garage in Peckham High Street was demolished in 1995-96 to make way for an extension to the Safeway store in The Aylesham Centre. The bus garage is included in *London Transport Bus Garages* by John Aldridge (Ian Allen Publishing). A photograph of it is among over eighty pictures in *Transport in Peckham and Nunhead* (South Riding Press). Pictures of the Bull Yard depot and the Peckham bus garage are shown in *Images of London: Peckham and Nunhead* (Tempus Publishing).

Other local titles published by Tempus

Southwark Remembered
JOHN D. BEASLEY

The current London Borough of Southwark was established in 1965, and consists of many civil parishes. Illustrated with over 100 old photographs, this volume documents the changing face of the area over the past 150 years, reveals the variety of life to be found in Southwark and recaptures the changes that have taken place in this most historic of London boroughs.
0 7524 2241 3

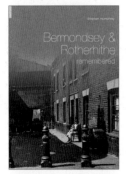

Bermondsey and Rotherhithe Remembered
STEPHEN HUMPHREY

There are few areas of London that have changed in recent decades as much as the dockside areas of Bermondsey and Rotherhithe. Drawing on the photographic collection held in Southwark Local Studies Library, this book recalls the days when these communities were at the heart of British commerce and industry. It also reveals the sights and sounds of an industrial heritage that is now all but gone.
0 7524 3316 4

Cinemas and Theatres of Wandsworth and Battersea
PATRICK LOOBEY

Cinemas and Theatres of Wandsworth and Battersea is an illustrated history bringing to life the places that occupied a warm place in the hearts of London's theatre-going public. This fascinating and informative gazetteer-style volume of the known venues in the area is illustrated with over 100 black and white images and contains a colour section of some of the area's best and brightest venues and advertisements.
0 7524 3356 3

London Life in the Post-War Years
DOUGLAS WHITWORTH

After the Second World War Douglas Whitworth took an important series of photographs of central London which reveal a city recovering from the trauma of conflict. These photographs show the extent of Blitz damage to famous streets and buildings, even in the very heart of the city, and illustrate how London looked as life began to get back to normal.
0 7524 2816 0

If you are interested in purchasing other books published by Tempus, or in case you have difficulty finding any Tempus books in your local bookshop, you can also place orders directly through our website
www.tempus-publishing.com